RETAIL'S LAST MILE

WHY ONLINE SHOPPING WILL EXCEED
OUR WILDEST PREDICTIONS

JONATHAN REEVE

ISBN 9780995410107 eISBN 9781925457360

Published by
Jonathan Reeve
www.jonathanreeve.com.au
jr@jonathanreeve.com.au

Printed in Australia
First edition: October 2016

Design and layout: Lorna Hendry
Editing: Jaclyn McRae
Cover illustration: Steph Hughes

RETAIL'S LAST MILE

WHY ONLINE SHOPPING WILL EXCEED
OUR WILDEST PREDICTIONS

JONATHAN REEVE

Jonathan Reeve is a speaker, author and adviser. He is passionate about helping retailers to build profitable, stress-free, online operations.

Jonathan has worked in retail businesses in the United Kingdom, the United States and Australia since 2001. He was part of the team that developed the operating model for Tesco.com, a global pioneer of online grocery retail. Jonathan's perspective is unique: he has both developed online retail strategy and led the frontline teams that deliver the service to customers. Jonathan has also worked in store retail and was the store manager of a large Tesco supermarket in London.

Jonathan has an MA in Economics from Cambridge University and an MBA with distinction from international business school INSEAD. Before setting up his own practice, Jonathan held roles with Aussie Farmers Direct and Coles Supermarkets in Australia, Tesco in the United Kingdom and the United States, and Goldman Sachs and Arkwright Consulting in the United Kingdom and Europe.

Jonathan lives in Melbourne with his wife Anna and sons Leo and Max. He enjoys keeping fit and has completed several ultramarathons and ironman triathlons.

CONTENTS

INTRODUCTION

I have written this book for those who want to stay ahead of the forces reshaping retail. As technology leads customers to shop in completely new ways, retail is undergoing a fundamental transformation and few players are ready for the changes ahead.

I have worked in online retail and store operations in the United Kingdom, the United States and Australia since 2001. I understand the strengths of store retail and am not naïve about the challenges facing online retail. That said, I have observed that the vast majority of retailers consistently underestimate the degree to which customers want to shop from home. They face a huge threat from disruptive retailers who have spotted the true opportunity and are solving the challenge of "retail's last mile": how to profitably sell and deliver products to customers shopping from home.

Throughout the developed world the rise of online retail has been consistent and relentless. In the United

States, which has the most accurate historical data, online retail's share of total spend has been growing at 15% a year since 2000, more than doubling in size every five years (see figure 1.1). Similar growth can be seen across most developed economies. I contend that as the delivery of products to consumers in their homes evolves to become truly efficient and convenient, online sales in developed economies will consistently grow at 10% per year and online will become the dominant shopping channel within 20 years. Even sectors such as groceries and fuel, where online currently takes just a small share of sales, are targets for disruption.

Figure 1.1
The relentless rise of online retail

US e-commerce share of total retail sales: 2000–2016

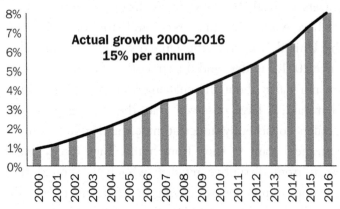

Source: *Estimated United States Retail Sales (Adjusted): Total and E-commerce* (United States Census Bureau, 2016).

Online retail's growth and impact on traditional store retail are not news. Almost every retailer is working hard to serve customers who want to shop in this way. Even so, the scale of the shift from stores to online is under-appreciated.

The history of retail since the emergence of the internet shows that following conventional wisdom is not a winning strategy. Long-term success has gone to those willing to think deeply about what their customers want and then take bold steps to deliver it.

WHAT'S COMING UP

The book is divided into three parts.

Part 1: **Why the last mile matters** examines why online retail is so powerful in addressing customer needs, and therefore has such huge potential. It describes the three mindsets retailers have adopted in responding to the online opportunity: passive, reactive and disruptive. It then sets out the biggest obstacle to online retail success – the last-mile challenge – how to profitably sell and deliver products to customers shopping from home. Part 1's main message is that online is set to grow massively and is only held back by the absence of profitable ways to deliver the products customers buy.

Part 2: **What is changing retail's last mile?** explains why the answer to the last-mile challenge is not so far off. Various innovations are contributing to two key developments that will crack the last-mile challenge –

smart digital decision-making and democratic delivery (cheap and convenient). I introduce a model in Part 2 that clarifies the relationship between these two essential components, describe the innovations that are changing retail as we know it, and forecast the potential for online in different product categories.

Part 3: **How to win the last-mile race** explores how retailers can solve the last-mile challenge. It sets out the three pillars of a successful online retail operation and highlights the business models that are best positioned to win, including my perspective on Amazon and its quest for total retail domination. The final chapter puts forward a systematic process for retailers to respond to the threat of online disruption and offers my outlook on the future of stores.

PART 1

WHY THE LAST MILE MATTERS

*People don't want to buy a quarter-inch drill.
They want a quarter-inch hole.*

THEODORE LEVITT, FORMER HARVARD BUSINESS SCHOOL
PROFESSOR OF MARKETING

CHAPTER 1

WHY CUSTOMERS WANT TO SHOP ONLINE

TESCO.COM'S LESSONS ABOUT PUTTING CUSTOMERS FIRST

My introduction to online retail was in 2001. I stumbled into the sector after my career had taken a wrong turn into investment banking and I was looking for an opportunity that did not involve working for a financial institution in the City of London. I got lucky. I was hired by a former Boston Consulting Group consultant turned retailer, Roy Perticucci, into an extremely smart team who were developing the operating model for Tesco.com, one of the pioneers of online grocery.

Although 2001 was early days for online retail, the idea for Tesco.com had come six years before. In 1995, two British grocery executives attended an Andersen Consulting (now Accenture) conference about the future of retail stores[1]. At this time, only 25% of households had

---

[1] Terry Leahy, *Management in 10 Words* (Random House Business, 2012).

computers. During the conference, a consultant predicted that in the future shoppers would order groceries using computers in their kitchens. The conference attendees nearly fell off their chairs laughing. But the Tesco executives – CEO, Terry Leahy, and marketing director, Tim Mason – later reflected on how convenient it would be for customers to have groceries delivered to their homes. As a result, they asked a small team to develop the United Kingdom's first grocery home-shopping application. The talented group made fast progress and in June 1996 Tesco Home Shopper was launched on CD-ROM to about 400 customers of the Osterley store in west London. Some 20 years later, Tesco.com has grown to sales of about GB£3 billion and is one of the few profitable online grocery retailers in the world.

Leahy and Mason's insight neatly captures a key message of this book. Although they led the United Kingdom's leading supermarket, operating several hundred stores across the country, they were able to put themselves in their customers' shoes and imagine a more convenient alternative to shopping for groceries in a store. They realised that many of their customers don't really want to spend their time walking up and down the aisles of a supermarket with a shopping trolley. It was just that they had no choice: a trip to the supermarket was the only cost-effective option for most of the population to acquire groceries.

THE THEORY OF DISRUPTIVE INNOVATION

The mindset of focusing on the jobs your customers really want taken care of, rather than your current business model, is the foundation of Clayton Christensen's theory of disruptive innovation. Christensen's body of work describes many examples of previously successful companies who spotted too late that a product innovation or new way of working had the potential to evolve and eventually disrupt their industry.

A classic story of disruptive innovation is the emergence of the steel mini-mills, which overtook the long dominant, integrated steel mills (a case study from Christensen's pioneering research and first book *The Innovator's Dilemma*[2]). Initially, mini-mills targeted the low end of the market with an inferior-quality product called rebar, suitable only for reinforcing cement used in construction. The leading integrated mills were happy to lose these customers since they were low profit. But the mini-mills slowly moved upmarket as their processes and products evolved and improved. Eventually, the mini-mills drove the previously dominant players to bankruptcy.

There are also disruptive consumer innovations that were mocked or a source of amusement when they first emerged but gradually evolved into a product we all take for granted. Steve Sasson invented the digital camera in 1975. The early prototype weighed almost four kilograms and the captured image was first recorded onto a cassette

2   Clayton Christensen, *The Innovator's Dilemma: When New Technologies Cause Great Firms to Fail* (Harvard Business Review Press, 2016).

tape, taking about 30 seconds to produce an image of 0.01 megapixels. Sasson worked for Kodak in the United States, at the time the dominant global player in photography, and few of his colleagues saw the potential of his invention. What Sasson foresaw, and almost all of his colleagues missed, was that his strange-looking invention had the potential to evolve and one day do a better and simpler job of capturing our memories than using film.

Figure 1.2
Steve Sasson, inventor of the digital camera,
with an early prototype

The challenge for any company is that there may be hundreds or even thousands of new innovations in their market each year. Many may be improvements, but which ones have the potential to overtake the established business model? Clayton Christensen's work provides two simple tests to apply.

The first test is whether the innovation addresses a fundamental problem some customers need solving. Often incumbent companies focus on improving the product or service they already provide, rather than taking a customer perspective and thinking about the underlying "job-to-be-done" and whether there is a better way for customers. This is the insight neatly captured in Theodore Levitt's quote at the start of this chapter: customers really want the hole the drill creates, not the drill itself. Too often, though, the existing players in an industry focus on improving the product they already sell, rather than thinking about the underlying customer need it meets and whether a completely different approach could better address it.

When thinking about jobs-to-be-done, it's vital to understand the needs customers have at different times and in different situations. Take a butcher. Some customers might visit a butcher with complete certainty about what they want to buy: perhaps they are preparing a meal for their family and know they need exactly six pork sausages. These customers just want the sausages as quickly and conveniently as possible. Other customers might have little idea what they will buy when they walk into the shop: perhaps they want to surprise their partner with an exotic new recipe for a special occasion. These customers are looking for inspiration and advice. The role of the butcher for each of these jobs-to-be-done will be different. All retailers need to understand the different needs of their customers and how well their business model meets them. Many traditional store retailers have been slow to recognise that home delivery could provide a better solution for some of their customers' jobs-to-be-done.

The second test is whether the innovator has what is known as an "extendable core". This is the secret sauce that allows the disruptive innovation to stay ahead as it moves into mainstream customer segments. It separates a disruptive innovation from a low-cost innovation. A contemporary example is the international expansion of discount supermarkets, such as Aldi from Germany. Whereas a mainstream supermarket might offer customers a choice of 20,000 to 30,000 lines, discount supermarkets such as Aldi focus on a curated selection of 1,000 to 2,000 lines that still meet their customers' needs. This simplicity allows Aldi to operate a lean business model and offer much lower prices than its full-range competitors.

When it entered new countries such as the United Kingdom and Australia, Aldi first targeted the lower end of the market. For this reason, it was often ignored by the dominant grocery retailers. Since establishing a foothold Aldi has been slowly moving upmarket and is now attracting customers from mainstream and even premium segments. Aldi's "extendable core" allowed it to retain its simpler business model while moving upmarket. It is now a serious threat to the established players.

ONLINE RETAIL IS A DISRUPTIVE INNOVATION

Online retail is a live case study in disruptive innovation. Delivery to the home will take off when it provides a better option to meet customers' jobs-to-be-done and, crucially, when retailers have recognised the opportunity and developed a model that successfully meets the need. The next chapter describes three different mindsets retailers have adopted in response to online retail, and explains why so few traditional retailers have successfully challenged their existing business model, even when it is in their customers' interests.

CHAPTER 2

ONLINE RETAIL: THE THREE MINDSETS

HOW RETAILERS HAVE RESPONDED TO ONLINE SHOPPING

In the many historical examples of disruptive innovation, incumbents often initially miss the importance of the new development because they are focused on improving products and services for the most profitable customers in their core market. This allows new entrants to gain a foothold in an overlooked or underserved segment, which incumbents ignore because of its low profitability. Gradually, however, the new entrants learn and move upmarket, leveraging the extendable core that gave them their early success.

I've written this book because, over my 15-year career in retail, I've repeatedly observed the vast majority of retail leaders fall into the same trap when faced with disruptive innovation. They continually underestimate the shift to online retail happening right in front of them. I first saw this in the early 2000s when most retailers adopted a passive approach to the first generation of online retail. Since online retailers were having little impact on the overall sales and profit of traditional stores, there was no impetus to change.

As online shopping steadily grew its market share in the 2000s, the trend towards online became impossible to ignore. Most retailers began shifting to a reactive strategy, responding to the changes in their market and developing their own online retail operations. However, these retailers were typically reacting to the happenings of now, rather than looking ahead to what customers would expect in the future. In such a fast-moving market this is still a high-risk strategy, even today. Only a very few retailers are taking the genuinely disruptive approach of thinking about what customers really need and developing a profitable long-term business model that delivers it.

Figure 2.1
The three online retail mindsets

MINDSET	ATTITUDE	FOCUS	PAY-OFF
Disruptive	"We're creating a new way for the future."	Future	5x
Reactive	"We're reacting to the world we see now."	Present	1x
Passive	"There's no need to adapt or change."	Past	0x

THE PASSIVE MINDSET

There have been many examples over the past 25 years of the passive mindset in online retail. Walmart is a classic illustration. In the late 1980s, Walmart became the world's largest retailer by sales and posted tremendous and seemingly unstoppable growth in the 1990s and 2000s.

In the United States it was far and away the dominant retailer when, in 2003, I moved to San Francisco to work for Safeway.com, which had started its own online grocery business in partnership with Tesco. On arriving in California, some eight years after the first deliveries of online groceries in the United States, I was surprised to discover that Walmart did not have an online grocery offer[3]. I could not understand how Walmart, with its vast resources and reputation for innovation, was not more focused on this revolutionary new way of shopping. In fact, Walmart only started properly testing the concept of home delivery of fresh groceries in 2011 with one trial in its home state.

Today, Walmart is making significant investments in an online grocery offering. In August 2016 it announced a US$3 billion acquisition of Jet.com, an online retailing startup with less than US$1 billion of gross sales and an unproven business model. Walmart is investing huge amounts of its shareholders' money to solve online grocery

---

3   Walmart did have a significant e-commerce business, with US$1 billion of sales in 2005. However, Walmart.com was focused on non-perishable lines such as electronics.

challenges that could have been addressed over 10 years ago if it had thought more deeply at the time about its customers' underlying needs.

Although Walmart has now moved on from its early passive mindset, this way of thinking can still be seen today among retailers in sectors that conventional wisdom believes are immune to disruption by online, for example, fuel and cars. The key message of this book is that there is a hidden threat for even these sectors: the reason online spend is still low in these sectors is not that customers love the existing ways of buying fuel or cars, it's simply that nobody has developed a convenient and efficient alternative.

THE REACTIVE MINDSET

Surely we are all now online or omni-channel retailers? Even the most diehard old-school retailers now operate online businesses, and the different channels to reach the customer are also increasingly integrated. Most mainstream retailers have the laudable aim of making it simple for their customers to shop for their full range of products how ever they like, through any channel they like.

But although almost every retailer is now taking online seriously, the vast majority are reacting to conventional wisdom, or what their competitors are doing now, rather than looking ahead to what their customers will expect in just a few years. Too often I see retailers who still under-estimate the impact of online because they focus on their current sales and profitability. They are missing the invisible threat of disruptive innovation. This is especially true of markets where companies such as Amazon are not yet operating. If the disruptors' efforts to solve the last-mile challenge are successful, and I believe some of them will be, there will be a catastrophic impact on most other retailers in the years ahead, with little chance of catching up.

THE DISRUPTIVE MINDSET

Only a few retailers have a genuinely disruptive mindset, which starts with the perspective that the underlying convenience of online retail is worthy of relentless pursuit. The most notable is, of course, Jeff Bezos, founder of Amazon, who left a well-paid investment banking job in the early 1990s because he believed in the potential of the internet to transform the way we shop (and in his own potential to lead that trend). What I love most about the story of Amazon is the way it has changed its business model several times to stay true to its ultimate purpose of being customer-centric.

In its early years, Amazon was a virtual retailer, operating out of Bezos's garage. It acted as an intermediary between book buyers and the large book distributors who owned the stock and had relationships with hundreds of book publishers. Over time, Amazon's model has evolved to the point where it now has one of the biggest inventory holdings of any retailer in the world: it flipped its business model because managing its own inventory became essential to its success as its range expanded. And it isn't stopping. Amazon is working to a bold ambition: to become "the everything store", able to offer every product a customer could need. If some customers prefer channels other than home delivery, Amazon will even look to find a way to meet their needs. In 2015 it acquired a property in Sunnyvale California that would allow a trial of drive-through pickup. In the United Kingdom it has been trialling lockers at popular rail stations. Bezos summed up his business model thus:

"We've had three big ideas at Amazon that we've stuck with for 18 years, and they're the reason we're successful: Put the customer first. Invent. And be patient."

JEFF BEZOS

THE PSYCHOLOGY OF DISRUPTIVE RETAILERS

The disruption of store retail by online is typically viewed using frameworks from business literature, such as Clayton Christensen's theory of disruptive innovation. Carol Dweck's classic book from the field of psychology *Mindset: The New Psychology of Success*[4] highlights that the

---

4 Carol S. Dweck, *Mindset: The New Psychology of Success* (Random House, 2006).

different approaches to online retail over the past 25 years also reflect our psychological mindsets.

Carol Dweck, a Stanford University psychologist, revealed two underlying mindsets in her research that describes how we, as individuals and groups, look at the possibility of achievement and success. She argues that people fall into either a "fixed" or a "growth" mindset. I see a clear application of Dweck's psychological mindsets to the world of retail and online.

Individuals and groups with a fixed mindset treat the world and our individual capabilities as fixed traits, with little potential for growth or development beyond a given level of innate ability. Contrasting this are those who possess a growth mindset and see human abilities as flexible and improvable through dedication and hard work.

Although the theory of fixed and growth mindsets was based on research into individual attitudes, it also captures well the different perspectives we see among retailers towards online. Some, like Leahy and Mason at Tesco, have consistently looked for opportunities to improve and adapt their models to a different future, demonstrating a clear growth mindset. Their attitude goes along the lines: *"home delivery looks like it would be great for our customers; let's see if we can find a way to make it work and make money"*.

Retailers with a fixed mindset, on the other hand, focus more narrowly on the situation right now. The attention of this group may be on the low profitability historically seen in online shopping, or the many inconveniences for customers in the online operations of today. They extrapolate that this will always be the case and this leads them to refrain from boldly attacking the opportunity. Walmart is an example of a retailer that for many years had a fixed mindset towards online retail, only realising its potential when new entrants such as Amazon had made the reality undeniable.

The problem with a fixed mindset is that it inherently limits innovation and experimentation, which is exactly what is needed in an environment undergoing disruption. The CEOs and executive teams of traditional retailers would do well to hold the mirror up to themselves and ask whether they are truly operating from a growth or a fixed mindset.

CHAPTER 3

OVERCOMING THE LAST-MILE CHALLENGE

WHAT IS THE LAST-MILE CHALLENGE?

The last mile is a challenge for almost every consumer business selling directly to the home. It goes beyond online retail. The term reflects that the final leg of the journey is the most costly and complex part of the operation. It was historically experienced in utility industries such as telecoms, electricity and water, which faced the challenge of building and maintaining physical infrastructure to link the distribution network to each customer's home. This part of the network, and associated activity such as individualised billing and customer service, added significantly to the cost of serving each customer and often made the difference between profit and loss.

There is an additional element in online retail that makes home delivery even tougher than in-store retailing. Before making the delivery, the online retailer has to pick and pack the product for the customer, whereas in a store the customer typically does this work themselves. Faced with this double-whammy of covering the cost of both picking and delivery, the first wave of online retailers started with a huge cost disadvantage relative to store retailers – often 15 to 20 percentage points of sales.

THE LAST-MILE CHALLENGE BEFORE THE INTERNET

To understand how online retailers are developing solutions to the last-mile challenge, let's consider how it was tackled before the birth of the internet. In the 20th century, there were many home delivery business models. The most popular were the daily delivery of staples such as newspapers and milk. In fact, some of these models survive to this day. This morning I have been reading a newspaper delivered directly to my front garden by someone who flung it out of a car window with one hand while steering a car travelling at 30 kilometres an hour with the other hand.

Two underlying reasons meant daily staple products could meet the last-mile challenge before the advent of electronic commerce: both the decision to buy and the delivery of the product were relatively simple to manage.

Firstly, the decision about what to buy only required occasional contact with the retailer to make a variation. As a child, I accompanied my father every few weeks to the local newsagent to pay in person for our newspapers and confirm the next set of deliveries, including alterations for any periods we would be away. The simplicity of this purchase process meant customers could leave a standing order in place with only occasional need to change it via a visit or phone call to the retailer.

Secondly, a localised logistics model to make a round trip of deliveries to a small catchment area can be extremely efficient. In fact, logistics professionals call this delivery model a "milk run". Because the person making deliveries of milk or newspapers might stop at almost every house in sequence on a street, this naturally creates an extremely efficient route. A busy milk round or newspaper delivery run in a typical suburb might make as many as 60 drops an hour. With little downtime between drops, the cost per delivery is extremely low.

Many of these business models experienced a steady decline in the '80s and '90s. In 1980, 89% of all milk in the United Kingdom was delivered to the doorstep. This share had fallen to just 3% of milk sales in 2015[5]. The rise of supermarkets and cheap groceries, and the labour costs of home delivery, made the business model unsustainable. Such home delivery models are reliant on high take-up to spread the largely fixed costs; once the customer base starts to decline it becomes harder and harder to survive as the reduced number of customers lowers sales but the fixed costs of the delivery run remain unchanged. Conversely, at high volumes, with several customers on the same street, these business models can be extremely profitable.

---

5   Harry Wallop, "On duty with the last of the milkmen" (United Kingdom
     Daily Telegraph, 22 January 2015).

THE IMPACT OF THE INTERNET

The emergence of the internet in the early 1990s changed everything for businesses that could deliver to the home and faced retail's last-mile challenge. The internet created the option for consumers to communicate electronically with retailers. This offered the possibility of ordering online from a retailer located anywhere. However, although the internet created a completely new option for consumers to place orders, it did nothing to change the second half of the equation: the physical challenge of last-mile delivery. Customers might have been able to order online but the products also needed to be conveniently and cost-effectively delivered. If the delivery part of the equation was not achievable the retailers would soon go out of business, either through low customer retention or unsustainably high costs.

THE LAST-MILE CHALLENGE IN BOOKS

The way this conundrum was solved in the early days of the internet was simple. The first sector to shift to online was one where the last-mile challenge was most easily solved: the product was suited to both purchasing online and delivering to the home. That product was books.

The first bookstores went online in the early 1990s. Cleveland-based bookseller Charles Stacks launched Book Stacks Unlimited, a website selling books, in

1992[6]. Stacks loved books and his motivation was the desire to offer customers access to half a million titles that could never be matched in a store. Then in 1994 Jeff Bezos created the early incarnation of what became Amazon, starting out in the garage of his house in Seattle on the west coast of the United States of America. Unlike Stacks, Bezos started selling books online not because he had a great love of them but because he analysed many different sectors and realised books presented the simplest opportunity to satisfy customers and make money with an online business model. As he later said[7]:

"Books are incredibly unusual in one respect and that is that there are more items in the book category than there are items in any other category by far."
JEFF BEZOS

By going online, Amazon offered customers the opportunity to browse a wider range of books, more quickly, and with more information to make a decision. So it met the first part of the last-mile challenge: it was simple to make a decision online. And books also had natural advantages for delivery. Because Amazon didn't own the stock it could provide a wider range of titles

---

6   Dustin Klein, "Visionary in obscurity: Charles Stack" (Smart Business Online, 22 July 2002).

7   Quoted in Steve Wasserman, "The Amazon Effect" (The Nation, 29 May 2012).

than its bricks-and-mortar rivals. And when it came to physical delivery, books were efficient to deliver because of their relatively small size and high value. Jeff Bezos had spotted the ideal conditions for an online tipping point. Book retail thus became the first sector Amazon entered.

WEBVAN AND THE LAST-MILE CHALLENGE FOR GROCERIES

Book selling was one of the first sectors to reach an online tipping point because it was inherently suited to home delivery. The rate of online take-up in most other sectors has been much slower. In fact, online has had minimal impact in some of the biggest retail sectors, including fuel, cars and groceries. This highlights that each sector faces a unique online tipping point; some markets may never see high online sales.

Consider the experience of online retailers in what is now known as the "dotcom boom" of the late 1990s. Many well-known online retailers were funded with the aim of disrupting sectors that Jeff Bezos would not have touched with the proverbial barge pole in those early days for online shopping. Webvan, founded in 1996, set out to revolutionise grocery shopping and had the backing of some of the smartest investors in the venture capital sector. George Shaheen, the CEO of Andersen Consulting (now Accenture), had quit his role to lead it. However, if Bezos had carefully handpicked the ideal sector for a pure-play online retailer, Webvan had chosen one of the hardest. It faced huge problems, some of its own making through expanding too quickly and not giving enough attention to how its team members would deliver the service. However, a hidden challenge was that its underlying profit formula just didn't add up: at low volumes, it's very hard to be profitable as a pure-play online grocery retailer. There is a significant cost in holding stock, especially the "long tail" of items that many customers need to have available but order infrequently. The cost of fresh food waste was also high for Webvan since there was no option to reduce the price of slow-moving perishable stock and sell it at a discount. Customers visiting a grocery store tend to perform much physical work: picking the items from the shelves, packing them up and then making the delivery to their own homes. Webvan took on all of this cost, including building a fleet of custom-designed refrigerated vans. Perhaps the biggest burden was the huge fixed cost associated with a centralised network of large purpose-built warehouses. After briefly reaching a peak valuation of US$5 billion in 2000, Webvan went bust just a few months later.

OTHER APPROACHES TO THE LAST-MILE CHALLENGE

A more successful approach developed in the early years of online retail was that of eBay. eBay acted as a virtual retailer, giving consumers the option to choose from a transparent comparison of potentially hundreds of different sellers who then organised delivery through the postal network. This proved a successful model, as customers were willing to accept the slower speed of the postal network when ordering products that were not urgently needed. For sellers, eBay's marketplace was an opportunity to sell stock that might otherwise have been marked down, or to reach previously untapped markets.

In the early dotcom era, several other delivery models emerged. In supermarkets and department stores, some of the early entrants followed Webvan and set up central distribution hubs. Others chose to use their existing stores as local distribution centres. There was also a raft of same-day delivery startups in the United States such as Kozmo and Urbanfetch, many of which soon went out of business due to the challenge of recouping the high costs of last-mile delivery. The key point is that every market segment starts in a different place: some, such as books, were already at the online tipping point. Other sectors, such as groceries, may take decades of hard work to reach a model that works for both consumers and retailers. Figure 3.1 shows the estimated share of online spend in different retail sectors in 2016. It highlights the huge difference between sectors in the propensity to shop online and the difficulty of solving the last-mile challenge. Tellingly, some sectors with low current online take-up present the greatest long-term opportunity for online. For example, grocery has huge potential for online shopping, mainly because most customers know in advance exactly what groceries they need to buy. However, most online retailers have struggled to find ways to profitably sell and deliver groceries to customers' homes.

Figure 3.1
Online take-up varies by sector

Estimated 2016 online share of retail sales by category
(G7 countries)

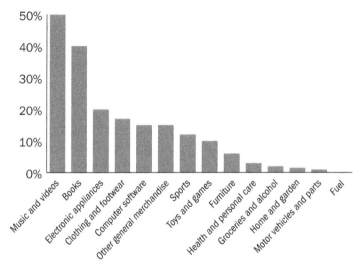

Source: Jonathan Reeve estimates of G7 average. Reported numbers
unavailable in this format, so estimates based on my own calculations
and experience.

CRACKING THE LAST-MILE CHALLENGE:
DECISION AND DELIVERY

In essence, online retail only takes off when customers
are happy with both key elements of the end-to-end
process: decision and delivery. I've seen that many online
retail businesses give disproportionate attention to
how customers will buy online and much less thought
to how the products will be delivered conveniently and
efficiently. But both are important, and it is often delivery

that has the greatest impact on customer satisfaction and retention, and also on the company's profitability. The disruptive Australian delivery service provider MeeMeep recently partnered with transport and logistics solutions provider, Blackbay, to survey Australian customers and understand the challenges facing online retail. The results showed that the biggest barriers to shopping online were mainly related to delivery.

Figure 3.2
Delivery issues are the main barrier to online shopping

MeeMeep and Blackbay survey:
What prevents consumers from shopping online?

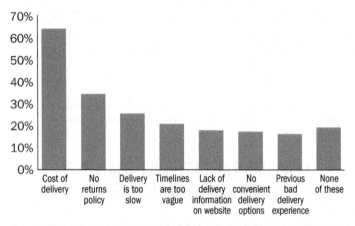

Source: Blackbay and MeeMeep. "2016 Online Delivery Report", available at www.blackbay.com/images/delivery-connect/BlackbayMeeMeepReport2016.pdf.

The distinction between "decision" and "delivery" forms the theoretical model that underpins this book. And cracking the last-mile challenge requires both these critical components, not dissimilar to a recipe with two essential ingredients, as illustrated in figure 3.3. It's not enough for just one to be present – retailers must both meet the digital user experience challenge (i.e. enable customers to make smart digital decisions) as well as the physical delivery challenge (i.e. achieve democratic delivery).

- Smart digital decision-making: it's **simple** for customers to make electronic purchases, **intelligent** systems help them take better decisions and customers can even **experience** what the product will be like before they buy.
- Democratic home delivery: customers have access to **cheap** and **convenient** home delivery.

Figure 3.3

Cracking the last-mile challenge is about decision and delivery

Decision vs. delivery matrix

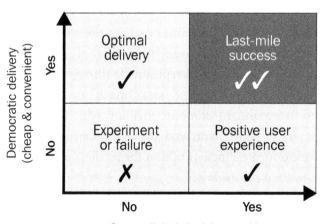

33

Let's use the example of books, which has already reached the top right quadrant of the matrix. Imagine you are looking online for a book on a hobby such as fly-fishing. To enable you to make a smart digital decision, book websites offer simple ways to assess the options by providing information on different books on the subject and their price and cost of delivery as well as advice to help you make a good choice. This might include an intelligent recommendation based on your previous purchases, the region where you live, or the books that other people with similar profiles tended to buy. We might also see ratings provided by other customers so you can see how previous readers ranked the different books on offer. The website might even allow you an experiential way of assessing the product, for example by allowing you to read an extract from the book. Once you've decided which book to buy, ordering should also be easy, potentially through "one-click" ordering.

After you've made the online purchase, the retailer must then offer a cheap and convenient method of delivery. In the case of books, this will typically be through the local postal network. The size of books means most can be posted in a standard domestic mailbox, which for most customers is convenient, and using the existing postal network is a cost-efficient option for retailers and allows them to keep prices down.

We can see how the last-mile challenge has been cracked in the case of books. Other retail categories, however, fall into different quadrants. For most customers, grocery shopping sits in the bottom right quadrant of the matrix. Online retailers have developed some smart tools for shopping for groceries online: for example, at the more innovative end of the spectrum, the Amazon Dash button that sits in your kitchen and allows you to re-order products (e.g. milk, bread) at the press of a button. However, very few online retailers, including Amazon, have yet cracked the physical delivery challenge of cheaply and conveniently getting groceries to your doorstep, especially fresh food items such as milk that need to be kept chilled.

Currently, very few retail sectors sit in the top right quadrant of the matrix. In fact, some of the biggest sectors, such as fuel and autos, are still firmly in the bottom left. Part 2 of this book describes the wave of innovation already underway that will solve the last-mile challenge and push many more retail sectors into the top right quadrant of the last-mile matrix in the years ahead.

PART 2

WHAT IS CHANGING RETAIL'S LAST MILE?

The world is moving so fast these days that the person who says it can't be done is generally interrupted by someone doing it.

ELBERT HUBBARD

CHAPTER 4

SMART DIGITAL DECISION-MAKING

The premise of this book is that an online tipping point will be reached in an individual retail sector when two critical components are present: smart digital decision-making (simple, intelligent and experiential tools to help customers make good product decisions) and democratic delivery (cheap and convenient delivery to the doorstep/location of choice).

We have already come a long way in the digitalisation of decisions and this is reflected in the way we buy products in stores as well as online. Recent surveys suggest that more than one-third of store sales are digital-influenced[8], where consumers have researched online before visiting the store, or even during their visit to the store. Many customers clearly still prefer to visit a store to finalise their purchase. Partly this is because of the home delivery challenge, but it's also because stores present many advantages over online when making a decision: perhaps there is a salesperson I

---

8   For example, *Navigating the Digital Divide* (Deloitte, May 2015).

trust, or I want the chance to try on clothes to check the fit and feel. However, there is a huge amount of innovation under way in the area of digital decision-making, which will shift customer preferences in favour of online retail.

THE THREE WAYS DIGITAL DECISION-MAKING WILL GET SMARTER

When we look at the decision process for buying a product online, there are three fundamental improvements underway:

- Simplicity: making it simpler for customers to research and buy the product.
- Intelligence: giving customers an informed opinion on the best choice.
- Experience: offering ways for customers to experience the product before they buy it.

There are myriad innovations underway in each of the three areas that are enabling consumers to make smarter digital decisions. Let's look at some of them.

SIMPLER DIGITAL DECISION-MAKING

To reach a decision about what product to buy, customers are looking to make a decision quickly and with access to relevant information. Innovations that simplify the buying process give customers the most relevant information at the time they need it, and then make it easy to buy.

REDUCING DECISION FATIGUE

There is increasing scientific evidence for the modern-day phenomenon of "decision fatigue". Consumers feel overwhelmed by the ever-expanding range of choices they face for almost every buying decision. And it's even having an impact on our mental health.

I realised this recently when shopping for milk at the local supermarket. As a child there was one variety of cow's milk: you could have any milk you wanted as long as it was full-cream. Now there are more than 20 varieties of cow's milk on sale, not including other options such as almond milk and goat's milk.

Online retailers are recognising the situations when offering consumers a restricted choice can make their lives simpler and create a deeper relationship that is hard for a competitor to break.

One such approach is the subscription model where customers commit in advance to an agreed regular level of purchases with a retailer. It's suitable when customers have highly predictable demand and are happy to be loyal to a particular retailer or service. Some early innovators in this area have been online clothing subscription services, including established players such as Trunk Club and Stitch Fix in the United States. Dollar Shave Club, a California-based online retailer, has taken a similar approach with razor blades and personal grooming products. It sends subscribers a monthly package of pre-ordered blades and other items in return for a fixed fee.

There are other benefits to subscription models: they are often tied to home delivery, but one of the biggest advantages is the reduced need for customers to spend time making decisions.

A slightly different situation is where consumers are loyal to a retailer or brand but demand is not predictable. A subscription model may not work here so the secret is to make it as simple as possible for the customer to reorder. A well-known innovation in this area is the Amazon Dash button. The Wi-Fi connected button sits in the home, allowing customers to reorder branded products as they run low. The product ordered is added to the next delivery Amazon is making to the customer's home.

Figure 4.1
Amazon Dash buttons for simpler ordering from home

Some appliance manufacturers are taking this a step further and building this capability directly into their products, for example the German company Brita has released smart water filters that can monitor the state of the filter and place an automated reorder for cartridges as they run low.

Reducing the number of decisions customers need to make doesn't just make their lives simpler. It also integrates the online retailer into customers' lives so they become more than just another product on the shelf. The key step for online retailers is spotting the opportunities in their customers' lives where choice has become a chore.

TRANSPARENCY: BE CHEAP OR BE UNIQUE

As a school student, my favourite subject was economics. I went on to study it at university. One of my first lessons was about the basic models of microeconomics. They were attractive to me because they made the world seem understandable and predictable.

However, some critics believe economic theory's predictability is based on flawed assumptions about the way the world works. For example, economic theory assumed "transparency", which meant that a potential buyer knew the quality and price of every product on the market. Back before the internet, this was rarely true except in a small number of markets for homogeneous products. The share market is an example.

Twenty-five years on and the world is very different. "Transparency" no longer looks like an academic pipedream. Why? Because of the huge amount of information accessible to consumers online.

Perhaps the clearest examples of transparency are online marketplaces. Go to eBay or any auction site, and search for a product. You will be presented with several potential suppliers along with an exact quote of the price of delivery. For those looking to compete successfully, there are really only two options: be cheap or be unique so nobody else can undercut or copy you.

The second example of price transparency is customer-driven price-checking. Using mobile devices, customers now have the ability to check prices for the same product online while they are shopping in a physical store, or a few minutes after leaving. It is a phenomenon more commonly known as "showrooming". How are retailers responding? The trick here is to embrace the change rather than fight it. Customers are going to compare different offers anyway, so put yourself in a stronger position by making it as simple as possible for customers to compare your offer.

Transparency impacts quality as well as price. There are now numerous review websites that let customers rate retailers on every possible criterion, from product quality to delivery speed. These sites open up a whole new perspective for customers, who can now access the wisdom of the crowd before buying a product. These sites keep retailers honest. There is no way to circumvent them – apart from having consistently good service and products.

Online retail is creating a world of increased transparency when it comes to price and quality. It's a world where poor quality or high price offers are quickly found out and efficiency and quality receive their reward. It is a tougher world. But it's a world that more closely resembles the ideal economic models of my studies.

SHOPPING ON THE GO WITH A MOBILE DEVICE

Giving customers access to information on their mobile devices doesn't give them access to more or better information. However, it does allow them to research and make decisions at times that suit them. Recent figures released by Google suggest that more than half of all searches now happen on mobile devices. So why does increasing mobile usage favour online retail? It becomes simpler for customers to research and shop in their downtime, for example while sitting on the sofa, or travelling to and from work. In isolation this trend is not enough to shift consumers online, but combined with other factors such as one-click ordering, it's driving a shift to simplify online shopping for customers.

MORE INTELLIGENT DIGITAL DECISION-MAKING

Digital innovation is also helping us make better, more intelligent, decisions. For example, over the past few years, we've seen a massive focus on personalisation, the trend to provide each customer with a tailored offer that works for them. Personalisation is set to get even more sophisticated and increasingly we won't even need to do the thinking for tasks that can be automated.

PERSONALISATION

Back in the early 1800s, before the Industrial Revolution and the advent of modern transport, most inhabitants of western civilisation lived in small rural communities. Everyone knew each other's personal information – not just names, birthdays, or hobbies – but also intimate information such as past relationships and even sexual orientation. The recent explosion in the public availability of personal data is returning us to those times, writes Harvard University fellow, Adam Tanner, in his 2014 book *What Stays in Vegas*[9]. Everything about an individual is known to the wider community, but that community now means corporates rather than individuals.

Tanner highlights the example of Las Vegas casinos, which push the use of personal data to extremes. For example, some casinos use retina recognition technology to personalise the behaviour of a slot machine to encourage gamblers to keep putting their dollars into a particular machine. However, the reality for most companies is that the personalisation journey is only just beginning and they are a long way from the wild-west frontier of Tanner's casinos. Most executives just need a simple approach to understand personalisation and get started.

It's worth noting the subtle distinction between personalisation and customisation. Customisation is when consumers nominate a particular set of features, for example the "large-soy-flat-white" you order at your

---

9   Adam Tanner, *What Stays in Vegas* (Public Affairs, 2014).

favourite coffee shop. Personalisation is when companies anticipate users' needs to create an individualised experience just for one person: for example, the barista starting to prepare your favourite coffee when you walk in the door if you're known to always order the same brew.

A simple framework is to think about three different types of personalisation: content, product and service.

Content personalisation is about predicting the content a customer is likely to prefer based on their past behaviour. Well-known digital examples are iTunes and Netflix, which serve up different content for every customer, based on their previous transactions (and also purchases that were not completed). The biggest challenge in using content personalisation for most non-tech companies is not a lack of data, but the ability to use and interpret it.

Service personalisation is still a novelty in most mass-market industries. Disney is a company leading the way with its Disney MagicBand, a personalised wristband with a 40-foot radio beacon: enter one of its restaurants in DisneyWorld in Florida and the greeter will already know your name and the kitchen will immediately start preparing the meal you preordered.

For those retailers offering home delivery, we're now seeing increasing opportunities to personalise deliveries to suit their customers. One example is a partnership between the car maker, Audi, and Amazon. In a current trial service in Munich, a courier will deliver goods directly to your parked Audi using a smart key that unlocks the car boot.

Product personalisation is already well under way. Footwear companies such as New Balance now offer mass personalisation. They can create shoes and clothes moulded exactly to a customer's body shape. This will be a huge boost to online retail, especially for repeat orders of personalised products once the initial fitting has been created.

Although clothing is already one of the biggest sectors of online retail, it is held back by the challenges of sizing. Without being able to try on an item in a fitting room there's a good chance that the product won't be a good fit and thus needs to be returned. Returns of clothing can run at 10-20% of items sold. This is expensive for the retailer and frustrating for the customer. It has proven to be one of the big obstacles to the take-up of online retail. We are already seeing the first wave of innovation as companies look to overcome this challenge. True Fit, based in the United States, offers a technology that matches your size with the sizing parameters of fashion labels that are likely to be known to the customer, reflecting that one company's size 14 may be very different to another's. Based on early results, True Fit claims an 18% reduction in the rate of returns in categories such as clothing and footwear.

MEET YOUR NEW VIRTUAL ASSISTANT

A group of software engineers in Silicon Valley in northern California recently ordered a pizza. Nothing unusual in that, except the order was placed on their behalf by "Viv", an artificial intelligence program which navigated the pizza company's automated ordering process and even selected the engineers' favourite toppings. The group included Dag Kittlaus and Adam Cheyer, two of the founders of Siri, the leader of the current generation of "virtual assistants" based on artificial intelligence platforms.

Kittlaus and Cheyer have spent four years developing Viv into a leader of the next wave of virtual assistants. These virtual assistants will perform routine tasks on our behalf: from ordering pizza to booking appointments and travel or cinema tickets.

The point for online retailers is that these virtual assistants are set to become your customers as sophisticated consumers start delegating hundreds of mundane tasks. We'll also start to see virtual assistants who are empowered to take decisions on the behalf of consumers. Forward-thinking retailers are already planning how they will participate by making it simple for virtual assistants to navigate their online stores.

Figure 4.2 highlights the three waves of artificial intelligence in retail and how we are about to transition from intelligent systems that think on our behalf to systems that can think and act on our behalf. The first wave of artificial intelligence in retail was the recommendation engine. Amazon's highly effective indirect approach – *"People who liked this book also bought …"* – has evolved to the point where sophisticated retailers now recognise cues and make proactive recommendations based on their access to so much of our information. For example, a bank might promote its foreign-exchange services after noticing a customer had bought tickets for an international flight.

The second wave of artificial intelligence is the one now under way: virtual assistants who can understand our instructions and perform basic tasks on our behalf. The breakthrough has come from the ability of these assistants to learn and recognise the hundreds of ways humans can deliver the same underlying message. Over time, we'll be talking more directly into our smartphones: not just to request information about a concert, but also to ask the virtual assistant to make the booking on our behalf.

Figure 4.2
Three waves of artificial intelligence in retail

Think vs. do matrix

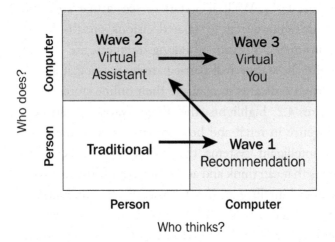

But there is a third wave of artificial intelligence that is yet to come: assistants who "think" and "do" on our behalf, as the model above shows. This "virtual you" will start as a virtual assistant, reordering basic grocery items for our homes, then will evolve as it learns from our behaviour to make complex decisions on our behalf. Imagine it's Friday and you've decided at short notice to go away for the weekend. You can't face trawling through travel websites so you might ask your phone: *"Find and book me the best hotel less than two hours away for Friday and Saturday nights."* "Virtual You" will know exactly what sort of hotel you liked in the past, your budget and even how the traffic on Friday evening will affect your travel times. Taking all this information, it could book the best option on your behalf.

Armed with this knowledge, some retailers are already starting to prepare now. They have recognised the importance of being able to interact with the current generation of virtual assistants and are making sure their online systems are virtual assistant-enabled. In the United States, the team behind Viv has already negotiated partnerships with more than 50 retailers with products ranging from food delivery to flowers. These retailers are setting themselves up for success by gaining early access to what is set to become a huge part of the market.

EXPERIENTIAL DIGITAL DECISION-MAKING

Perhaps the most oft-cited reason for the continued dominance of store retail is the simple fact that stores provide an opportunity to experience the product before buying it. The best experience most online retailers can offer has historically been an image of the product on the website, possibly a video. A technology that will have a profound impact in changing this distinction is virtual reality.

eBay and the Australian retailer Myer recently launched the first virtual reality department store. Anyone with a headset or glasses and a downloaded app could browse departments as though they were in a physical store.

Figure 4.3
Virtual reality retail will soon be a reality

Photo from the Australian launch of the Myer and eBay virtual reality department store.

We are also seeing the first generation of virtual fitting rooms that allow the customer to try on an item and vary the colour or background imagery to see how it will look. It's only a matter of time before we'll be able to get a virtual indication of exactly what a product will look like on our own body without needing to try it on. Of course, this won't be the same as trying it on in a store fitting room and seeing it in the mirror, but it will be a huge advance on where we are today and another step to close the gap between online and store retail.

In this chapter, I've highlighted many ways that technology is evolving to allow customers to make smart digital decisions. In fact, I expect digital decisions could increasingly do a better job of anticipating our needs and how to meet them. On its own, the digitalisation of decisions is not enough to increase the popularity of home delivery – often it's equally compatible with shopping in stores. But when combined with convenient and affordable delivery, it creates the conditions for an online tipping point as the customer no longer needs to visit the store. The next chapter sets out the big trends making delivery more convenient and affordable that will lead to many more customers shifting to online.

CHAPTER 5

DEMOCRATIC DELIVERY

A STEP CHANGE IS NEEDED

The second critical ingredient for solving the last-mile challenge is being able to offer consumers cheap and convenient delivery options. I call this "democratic delivery" to reflect that online shopping will only reach its full potential when delivery is accessible to all customers, not just the few who can afford high delivery fees or are willing to put up with inconvenient service.

Although cheap and convenient delivery is close to being realised in a few sectors, for example books, for most it is still a long way off and striking the right balance between cost and convenience is a huge challenge. Indeed, the majority of current online delivery models are unprofitable. However, we are now seeing a wave of innovation aimed at overcoming the obstacles, as more players gear up for the last-mile challenge. Figure 5.1 illustrates the typical online retailer's path towards

Figure 5.1
A step change in efficiency is needed to reach online profitability

Typical online retail operating model efficiency

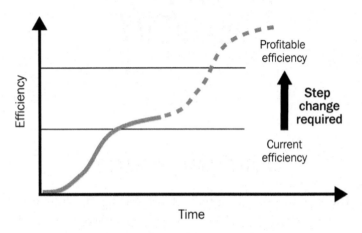

achieving efficient fulfilment for its online operation. Most players are making incremental steps towards lower cost, but to make the leap to profitability a step change is still needed. It is hard to make money delivering to the last mile and my own experience suggests most online retailers are still five to ten percentage points away from sustainable profitability.

Even Amazon, the undisputed global leader in online retail, has barely made a profit in its retail operation during its entire history. This is mainly due to its huge cost of distribution. The only reason Amazon survived in its early years was thanks to a well-timed capital-raising of US$2.2 billion at the peak of the dotcom investor mania. Fast-forward to 2016 and Amazon, together with most other online retailers, still faces the same profitability gap. While its fulfilment is more efficient, free shipping is now ubiquitous. Indeed, Amazon had a net deficit on shipping of US$5 billion in 2015 and this continues to drive the company's low overall profitability – less than one cent on every dollar of sales.

Many observers doubt that pure-play online retail can ever be profitable and assert that in the long-term store retail will retain its dominance. It has been a frequent observation of one of the most prominent commentators on online retail, Stern School of Business Marketing Professor Scott Galloway[10]:

"The Achilles heel of Amazon and other pure-play online players is solving for the last mile. Last year, Amazon spent $6.6 billion on delivery and received $3.1 billion in shipping fees. For consumers as well, high delivery speeds and low-cost shipping options are often outweighed by the burden of being at home to receive packages."
SCOTT GALLOWAY

What many commentators ignore in their commentary on profitability is that disruptive innovation is a process, not a static situation. Amazon is making a long-term play for profitability.

---

10 Scott Galloway, "The Future of Retail Looks Like Macy's, Not Amazon" (LinkedIn, May 2015).

In the rest of this chapter I describe various innovations that will democratise home delivery, by making it both more efficient (thereby allowing online retailers to price their services more cheaply) and more convenient.

EFFICIENCY THROUGH ECONOMIES OF SCALE

One of the big challenges for the pioneers in online retail in the 1990s – which still persists today – is that the fixed costs of last-mile fulfilment are extremely high. Added to this is the double-whammy that costs are incurred in two very different activities: the cost of picking and packing the items and the cost of making the final delivery. With high fixed costs and low margins, economies of scale are often critical to profitability.

BENEFITS OF SCALE IN PICKING

When it comes to scale, online is taking retail to a whole new level. Amazon's mega fulfilment centres are now some of the biggest warehouses in the world, taking up more than 1 million square feet of space, with workers getting around them on bicycles. These fulfilment centres are the foundation hubs of Amazon's last-mile strategy, with millions of orders every week funnelled from customers through to a vast network of conveyors, ramps, totes, storage bins and several thousand team members.

These centres don't just fulfil Amazon's own orders. More than 40% of Amazon's sales are now "Fulfilled by Amazon" on behalf of the supplier. This gives Amazon a further advantage because it can offer customers a much longer tail of products and it gets more volume to process, spreading the fixed costs and enjoying the benefits of greater scale.

BENEFITS OF SCALE IN DELIVERY

The second activity where scale makes a difference is delivery. The most efficient domestic distribution businesses operate close to an old-style "milk run" delivery schedule, delivering sequentially to homes in close proximity. Conversely, the worst distribution efficiency comes when there are only a few orders and they are located in different parts of a large town or city. As figure 5.2 illustrates, there is a direct link between the number of customers and the average distance between each customer.

This was the challenge facing many of the early online retail pioneers and it created a decision trap: minimise costs by scheduling fewer trucks to cover the entire city or minimise complaints by scheduling more trucks to hit the promised customer service levels?

There are a few ways to improve delivery economics by encouraging customers to behave in particular ways; for example, incentivising customers in the same neighbourhood to order at similar times. Over the long-term the simplest way to reduce cost and improve service

Figure 5.2
Increasing customer numbers improves delivery efficiency
Illustrative delivery catchments and customer numbers

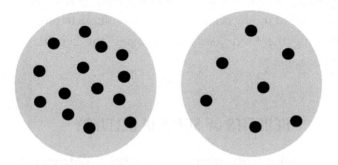

is scale. If 15 customers in one neighbourhood all have drops scheduled for one afternoon, then routing becomes simple because just one truck can be scheduled. This situation also makes it efficient to add new customers because the marginal cost of the extra customer is low. This is where Amazon is heading with its subscription service: achieving huge scale allows you to attract additional customers with aggressive pricing because the chances are you will be in the area anyway. Amazon's scale has now allowed it to reach a point where it is introducing its own local fulfilment centres. Although costly to run, these add another advantage discussed in more detail later: speed. Amazon uses these centres to deliver its Prime Now service, which promises free two-hour delivery in urban areas on a wide range of staple items. This is only possible at a scale where Amazon has a huge customer base willing to pay for the service and make it profitable even on low margins.

In summary, as more and more customers opt for home delivery in the way they shop, the cost of providing the service is subject to a natural economy of scale. Although the examples here relate to online retailers with their own distribution networks, the benefits of scale equally apply to third-party logistics providers.

EFFICIENCY THROUGH AUTOMATION: THE ROBOTS ARE COMING

Just as the benefits of scale can drive down costs in both fulfilment and delivery, so can automation. Picking and delivering products can be labour-intensive. It is not unusual for salary costs alone to account for 15-20% of sales in an online retail business. Automation is a way around this.

PICKING AUTOMATION

One example of automation is in the fulfilment operation; in particular, the use of conveyors and automated picking. John Lewis, one of the online retail leaders in the United Kingdom, made a huge investment in an automated fulfilment centre that serves both its store and online customers. This has been a major factor in its success as an omni-channel retailer that leads the way with customers who shop both in stores and online. Likewise, Amazon has made inroads with automation and in 2012 bought

Kiva Systems, one of the leaders in warehouse robot technology. It is now using Kiva robots to perform many of the repetitive tasks in its fulfilment centres.

DELIVERY AUTOMATION

The use of automation in the delivery stage already has a high profile thanks to well-publicised trials of delivery drones and driverless cars. These are making headlines as potential innovations to solve the last-mile challenge. Conventional wisdom would tell us that these solutions come with insurmountable obstacles, such as safety considerations in built-up areas, and will never play a central role in fulfilment.

I'm not so sure. Disruption is a long-term process and the key consideration is whether an innovation meets a fundamental customer need. Automated delivery systems such as driverless cars and drones certainly meet a huge customer need: the desire for low-cost home delivery. My bet is that a wave of improvements and refinements to automated delivery will beat the last-mile challenge and that drones and driverless cars will be a big part of the solution to online retail's profitability gap.

What these innovations illustrate is that a few companies are on course to address and solve the last-mile challenge. Despite this, most retailers are, in the meantime, still working on fixing the basic operational processes of getting products to the doorstep.

DELIVERY CONVENIENCE AND THE NEED FOR SPEED

We are also seeing a wave of innovation at the end of the chain as retailers simplify the process by which customers receive their products. Historically, a major drawback of many online purchases for the customer was the need to be at home to accept the delivery. If the delivery was missed, the customer had to traipse to the local post office or arrange a redelivery. This also added significant cost to the distributor. We're now seeing many innovations to address this, from lockers on the doorstep to a trial of in-fridge delivery (explained below). As well as making it more convenient for the customer, the best initiatives also reduce the cost to the retailer.

WHEN DOORSTEP DOESN'T CUT IT: THE SHIFT TO ULTRA-CONVENIENT DELIVERY

In Sweden, a consortium of three companies is piloting a world-first service allowing customers to order groceries online and have them delivered directly to their fridge. For security and tracking, customers must have a digital lock on their front door that can be opened by the delivery driver using a smartphone. Deliveries can be made when the family is away from the home, so the service removes all physical effort linked to grocery shopping.

The problems we see customers experiencing with existing home delivery models are what holds back the growth of online retail. Doorstep delivery in its current form can be frustrating for customers and retailers alike. We all know the hassles of arranging redelivery when one is not home at the time of first delivery. Indeed, Blackbay and MeeMeep's recent survey in Australia showed that 44% of online shoppers had had to wait at home between four hours and a day for delivery.

New approaches attempt to address the being-at-home challenge. These range from making it simpler to arrange a redelivery, to positioning lockers at busy transport hubs. These help, but they do not always address the cause of the problem. What many customers want is right-first-time delivery to the home, but they settle for another option when that isn't available, or when something goes wrong.

Many customers will have concerns with the idea of unattended deliveries being made to their fridge, but still, I'm a fan of the concept because it's a bold attempt to address directly the core need most customers have: I want my products to arrive at my house in a convenient way.

Smart retailers are looking for ways to make home delivery simpler. The first step is to realise that near enough may no longer be good enough; new solutions are on their way and every online retailer needs to be aware of them. It's a matter of looking at the most common problems customers face and working out what they really want. In-fridge delivery is one example of this, but there are many other solutions that will work for other online retail models: from centralised lockers at popular urban locations to local distribution centres that hold the product until customers return home. All these and more are being developed and trialled as retail moves from stores to the streets.

THE NEED FOR SPEED

Amazon has put speed at the heart of its online retail offer. In the United States, as mentioned earlier, it recently introduced Prime Now, a city-based local delivery service with a two-hour delivery window. We're also seeing a new generation of ultra-fast delivery companies in sectors such as meal delivery. Hundreds of bike and motorbike couriers now criss-cross most cities every evening, racing to get meals delivered within an hour of the order being placed.

But how important is delivery speed to most customers and how does it affect the profitability of the retailers considering speedier delivery options? The premise of Amazon's strategy is that consumers prefer speedier delivery and over time, the quickest will win. But does that hold true? I learned a long time ago in retail that there's no such thing as an "average" consumer; just lots of different segments. A good way to look at this question is by breaking it down to look at the underlying needs of different customer segments.

One clear segment of demand is for urgent deliveries. It's 7pm after a long day at work and you've just realised there's nothing in your fridge. A 45-minute delivery from your favourite restaurant can look very attractive. This drives the business model of hyper-local food delivery services, such as Deliveroo and Delivery Hero. These firms may allocate deliverers to a single suburb to ensure customers receive their orders as quickly as possible.

At the other extreme, there are products which customers are likely to be indifferent about receiving earlier. If I've ordered a staple item such as flour or sugar and already have enough in my home to last a few days, I'm probably unwilling to pay for a delivery to arrive earlier. It's more important that I can arrange when the delivery will arrive so I know I will be home to receive it.

Between the two extremes are discretionary items: for example, a new dress or a pair of jeans ordered as a treat. This is where there is a huge variation in delivery speeds. For a wanted item, it's likely the customer will prefer to receive it sooner even though they may be unwilling to pay much of a premium. Other things being equal, the speedier retailer is likely to come out on top in the long run.

So what does this mean in practice and can retailers focus on just one approach? In reality, most consumers will switch depending on the situation, even for the same product. I may be happy with a long lead-time for flour most weeks, but if it's Friday and I need more flour for a cake I'm baking on Saturday then only next-day delivery will work. To keep their customers happy, retailers need to be able to flex their delivery offer to suit their customers or risk them moving away when their needs change. The challenge for online retailers is that many already lose money. How can they find ways to increase speed without increasing costs? Are there ways to increase speed whilst also reducing costs?

THE CHANGING RELATIONSHIP BETWEEN SPEED AND COST

The link between speed of delivery and cost for an online retailer has traditionally followed a simple inverse relationship. Customers were offered a standard option, perhaps via the postal network, a more expensive express option, and, if it was logistically possible, a same-day or next-day option with the highest price. Earlier today I used one of Australia's leading online bookstores and was offered two options for delivery:

• Standard delivery for A$6.95
• Express delivery for A$14.95 (ships next day)

There was no option for same-day delivery, presumably because it is logistically impossible or would be prohibitively expensive. The traditional inverse link between speed and cost is shown in figure 5.3, with cost increasing sharply for shorter delivery times.

The reality for most online retailers is that they have been using logistics models designed before the advent of online shopping. We are now seeing the emergence of a new generation of logistics models, developed in response to the growth of online shopping, in which speed is given much greater importance. The holy grail of these models is to offer a same-day delivery option which is cheaper than or the same cost as multi-day delivery. Impossible? Let's look at a couple of examples.

Figure 5.3
Traditional inverse link between speed and cost of delivery

Cost vs. speed of delivery

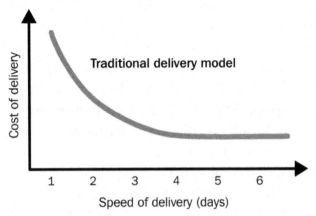

THE "NATURAL MONOPOLY" MODEL

Some online retailers who found the traditional logistics providers unable to meet their delivery needs have set up their own delivery network. This is the approach adopted by most online grocery retailers who need to transport fresh produce as quickly as possible to customers' doorsteps. It's also a large and increasing element of Amazon's fulfilment strategy in both the United States and Europe.

Setting up your own network is both costly and complex (as I know myself from my time managing a Tesco store that had its own fleet of delivery vans). However, once the infrastructure is in place it also confers huge benefits on the owner of the network, one of which is speed. Imagine a retailer already has a delivery truck scheduled to visit your suburb tomorrow. If you place a new order then the marginal cost of adding your delivery is low, even though the retailer is offering a next-day delivery service.

I call this a "natural monopoly" strategy because it's similar to railways and utilities – as soon as one company has laid down the expensive infrastructure and built scale it's very hard for other companies to compete. There is a tremendous first-mover advantage in getting there first.

VIRTUAL NETWORK

At the other end of the scale is a new breed of virtual delivery networks, such as Deliv in the United States and MeeMeep in Australia, who do not own any of the underlying physical assets. Instead, they have developed proprietary models to co-ordinate buyers and sellers to achieve the most efficient result. Many of these models are examples of the sharing economy, drawing on under-utilised assets (for example couriers with downtime between scheduled jobs) to create a cost-effective on-demand delivery option.

There are a couple of keys to success for these virtual models to achieve cost-effective same-day or next-day delivery. Although the approach can look like a classic example of a completely free market, in fact a level of co-ordination is beneficial. Deliv in the United States has built a first-mover advantage with mall-based retailers who want to offer same-day local delivery to customers.

By partnering with several retailers in one mall it gains economies of scale, because Deliv's nominated driver can pick up multiple deliveries at the same time. Some mall owners even co-ordinate the collection of deliveries to make the process as simple as possible for their retailers and Deliv.

Another key to success is quality control. MeeMeep in Australia has a feedback system, similar to Uber's rating system for its drivers, which allows customers to report on delivery performance. MeeMeep can then offer a reliable out-sourced network that ensures the required quality of service for its customers.

WHAT ABOUT TRADITIONAL DELIVERY AND POSTAL NETWORKS?

There are already existing networks making deliveries daily to different neighbourhoods, most obviously the national postal networks. Why can't these also compete in the battle for ultra-efficient same-day delivery? In theory, they can and they have a huge head-start. However, in most countries, these large and often state-owned companies have found it extremely challenging to adapt their culture and business models to meet customers' new requirements.

CASE STUDY: HOW SANTA CLAUS BALANCES CONVENIENCE AND EFFICIENCY

A wave of innovators, from Instacart to Uber, is bringing fresh approaches to the last-mile problem. But we can also learn from someone with a much longer track record in last-mile delivery: Santa.

One of the biggest problems for online retailers is that the well-intended desire to offer customers a choice about the time of delivery also significantly raises costs. Same-day delivery can be a particularly expensive variant of this phenomenon. There are many examples of bankrupt online retailers who learned too late that offering customers a great service is not a winning long-term strategy if you can't make money at the same time.

Santa Claus has a unique strategy for creating an efficient delivery schedule. By delivering to every house on the planet on only one day each year he keeps his "wasted" time between drops to a minimum. The genius of Santa's business model is that his customers don't think their choice has been restricted: in fact, they prefer to all receive their deliveries on the same day.

Another tricky part of the last-mile problem is that customers may need to be at home to receive their deliveries. It adds cost to the transaction for the retailer and time and effort for the customer. In my experience, this is one of the biggest barriers to the growth of online retail.

Again, Santa has figured this out. By delivering through the chimney when his customers are asleep Santa doesn't need to worry about waiting for someone to answer the doorbell and then sign for the package, or even how to arrange a redelivery if the customer isn't home. And by leaving the delivery right where it will be opened on Christmas morning he's making life even simpler for his customers.

What we learn from Santa is that there can be smart ways to offer convenience and also improve efficiency at the same time.

CHAPTER 6

HOW BIG COULD ONLINE RETAIL BECOME?

WHAT'S IN A NAME?

I believe there is misunderstanding about the forces driving online retail, and therefore its future growth, due to the names we use to describe it. For the past 25 years, the preferred name for the new form of retail unleashed by the internet has been "online retail" or "e-commerce". Yet these names only tell half the story and disproportionately preference the technology-driven aspect of this way of shopping. "Online retail" accurately describes the digitally-enabled decision to buy. But it does not reflect that in 90% of cases the subsequent deliveries to the home use a traditional logistics model. The growth of "home delivery" would be an equally valid way to describe the trend that "online retail" represents.

Equally, "e-commerce" is often seen as a technology change but driving its growth, or otherwise, is the logistics challenge of conveniently and efficiently getting products to the doorstep. As described in Chapter 3, it is only when both challenges are solved that we see a tipping point occur. Often, it is the physical delivery challenge that holds back online retail or e-commerce more than it is technology. As innovation breaks down the barriers to efficient delivery I contend that we will see online retail continue its relentless growth.

In the preceding chapters, I've highlighted several different innovations that will combine to break down the barriers to retail's last mile. However, of these, there are two changes that will dominate in terms of impact: same-day delivery and automation.

CHEAP SAME-DAY DELIVERY WILL CREATE AN ONLINE TIPPING POINT

The impact of cheap same-day delivery on online retail will be indirect but profound. Same-day delivery will open up the grocery sector to online shopping, leading to a massive expansion in the physical infrastructure supporting home delivery. This in turn will fuel the growth of products in other categories as a virtuous circle is established where scale drives home delivery to become cheaper and more convenient.

The impact of same-day delivery is under-estimated because it's not something many customers are currently demanding or willing to pay for. However, as Henry Ford (allegedly) observed, *"If I had asked people what they wanted, they would have said faster horses."* Most online sales today are in sectors where speed of delivery is typically unimportant. Grocery is different: most of us make at least three shopping trips a week for groceries, often buying small baskets of goods on which online retailers are unable to make a profit delivering to the home. How could things be different? Imagine it's breakfast time and you notice you're running low on milk. You issue a request for more milk to the voice-activated console sitting on your kitchen bench, which is in regular communication with your preferred online grocery retailer. As milk is a staple, the online retailer's system automatically schedules a delivery for the same afternoon, on a truck that is already making several drops in your neighbourhood. To ensure the delivery is profitable it also adds a few other grocery products its systems predict your household will need in the next week. The entire order is delivered to a refrigerated locker on your doorstep during the day, ready and waiting when you return home.

As consumers become locked into ordering for same-day delivery, which can be offered at a reasonable price if the online retailer has the scale to operate daily trucks in every neighbourhood, this will create the delivery infrastructure for the majority of us to shop online regularly and consistently. Grocery accounts for 15-20% of retail spend in most developed economies and much of this is predictable. As discussed in the next chapter, this shift will create huge natural economies of scale for the retailer who can win the online grocery race.

I hear some retailers argue that their customers don't place much value on speed, perhaps because customers are now unwilling to pay a premium for faster delivery. This is a dangerous assumption. In Chapter 5 we saw how new models of delivery are pushing innovation that will reduce the cost of delivery for same-day or next-day delivery. You can see this in figure 6.1. As models emerge that are able to deliver products on the same day – at costs similar to or lower than your multi-day options – customers are always going to choose the faster option. All the better if their life is simpler because they have the confidence to consolidate their orders for different product categories with one online retailer. By that point it will be very hard for retailers who have not kept up with the pace of innovation to adjust their model and compete with cheap same-day or next-day delivery.

Figure 6.1
Innovation is bringing down the cost of same-day delivery

Cost vs. speed of delivery

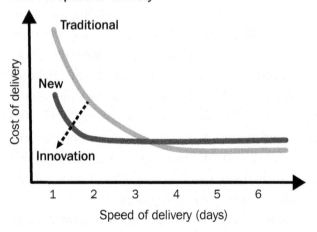

AUTOMATION WILL DRIVE DOWN COST AND INCREASE AFFORDABILITY

Automation will also have a profound impact because of its potential to dramatically reduce the cost of last-mile fulfilment. Most current online retail operations are highly labour-intensive with over 20% of sales typically incurred in direct labour costs. However, many of the tasks completed are simple and repeated, for example picking products in warehouses. This makes them ideally suited to automation.

To illustrate how the cost of last-mile delivery hinders the growth of online retail, let's reflect on a sector where online has had a negligible impact: fuel for personal cars and vehicles. Is it that customers like and choose the experience of shopping for their fuel in person at the gas station? I've asked this question of many people and typically they say that what keeps them shopping at gas stations is not the service or brand loyalty, it's simply that there is no other cost-effective and convenient alternative. In fact, most people have not even considered there could be an alternative. Most surveys of online retail exclude fuel as a category even worth measuring.

The absence of a widespread fuel home delivery model is not really due to the challenge of digital decision-making. In fact, it would be simple to create an app that allows customers to request a delivery of fuel. The market is held back because the costs of solving the last-mile challenge make it tough to generate a return on the investment needed. Transporting fuel is expensive (partly because of all the safety requirements); it can be hard to schedule access to an unattended car and the margins on fuel are low in the first place. So what holds the sector back is the challenge of making a profit on a last-mile delivery model, not customer satisfaction with the current model.

COULD PETROL STATIONS BE DISRUPTED BY THE DELIVERY OF FUEL TO THE CAR?

Yes, indeed they could. Fuel is a classic disruption opportunity because the current way of buying it is a task most customers find inconvenient and don't enjoy. Disruption will happen when a new player starts with a very basic service and then slowly over time refines and improves it until eventually it has an offer that works for customers and makes money. I believe that at some point in the future a direct to car fuel delivery model will emerge that is founded on intelligent technology that alerts a retailer when one's car is running low on fuel (smart digital decision-making), and a cheap and convenient way to enable the retailer to gain access to one's fuel tank when one is not present (democratic delivery). The key to making this disruption cost-effective will be automation in parts of the process, for example through self-driving vehicles navigating parts of the process.

What might things look like in 20 years? Imagine your car can recognise when it's fuel tank is less than one-quarter full and issue a request to be filled up at the next opportunity. You might leave your car in a city car park while on a shopping trip. While you're away your car self-drives to a designated area in the car park where it is filled by a fuel company team member who is permanently assigned to the car park. The car then drives to a different parking spot and you are notified of the transaction and the payment that has been charged automatically to your credit card. You are also sent a map and route to the location of the car's new parking spot. This scenario is achievable with technology available today. It would open up a huge percentage of the conventional fuel market to disruption, especially in urban areas.

WHERE WILL IT END UP?

Since 2000 the estimated share of online retail in most western economies has grown from negligible levels to an average of 7% of total retail sales, and as high as 10% in the United Kingdom. I contend that innovation enabling customers to make smart digital decisions and facilitating cheap and convenient delivery will propel online to continued consistent growth of over 10% per year. And as the barriers holding back online shopping are overcome, it will become the dominant shopping channel within 20 years.

One of the complications of predicting the growth of online retail is that the challenges are so different by sector. It can be dangerous and misleading to base forecasts on the average current take-up when some sectors, such as music and books, are already at high levels of online sales with limited growth potential. Equally, the share of online sales is close to zero in other sectors and there may be good reasons it can never increase significantly.

I have taken a point of view and forecast the share of online in different retail sectors in 2036 (20 years from the publication date of this book). The forecast is based on the current share of online sales and my review and analysis of how innovation in digital decision-making and physical delivery will impact each sector. My estimate of the sector's long-term potential is driven by the characteristics of each sector including:

Smart digital decision-making
- Predictability of demand
- Share of repeat purchases
- Importance attached to experiencing the product in the decision process
- Typical returns ratio

Democratic delivery
- Absence of restrictive consumer or producer regulations
- Share of costs associated with distribution
- Potential for automation of key tasks

Although the sectors with already high levels of online penetration will still lead the pack, I believe we will see the biggest growth in sectors that currently have very low levels of online penetration such as grocery and fuel. These have characteristics which are highly supportive of online retail, in particular the dominant model today is often perceived as inconvenient by customers. In each case there is innovation already underway, highlighted in the book, which can overcome the existing barriers to online take-up.

Figure 6.2
Online's share of spend is projected to increase in all retail sectors

Estimated 2036 online share of retail sales by category (G7 average)

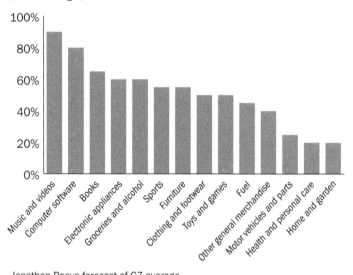

Jonathan Reeve forecast of G7 average.

THE WORLD WAKES UP TO ONLINE RETAIL'S TRUE POTENTIAL?

As I write this in late 2016, it seems many other observers have started to realise the massive disruptive potential of online shopping, especially in the United States. There are many indicators of this, but perhaps the most telling has been Amazon's share price growth. More and more investors have realised that Amazon could be the first retailer to crack the last-mile challenge.

Figure 6.3
The market recognises Amazon's disruptive potential

Amazon stock price: 1997–2016

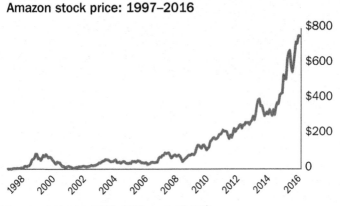

Amazon stock price 1997–2016, quoted in US$.

In the next chapter, I look at how Amazon and other business models plan to win the race to the doorstep and how incumbent retailers can best respond.

PART 3

HOW TO WIN THE LAST-MILE RACE

Thinking is the hardest work there is, which is probably the reason why so few engage in it.

HENRY FORD

→ CHAPTER 7 ←

THE THREE PILLARS OF ONLINE RETAIL SUCCESS

Today's online retail challenge is different to many other problems retail leaders will face in their careers because it is both new and unique. The disruption of store retail by online will only happen once in our lifetimes and there is no textbook or prior experience we can draw upon. Approaching the online challenge calls for some deep thinking on the part of retailers to develop an offer that both works for customers and is profitable. And once the business model is conceived it must then be successfully implemented, often by team members who have never worked in this way before. This is no small challenge and the history of online retail over the past 25 years is littered with the corpses of retailers who did not get it right.

Jeff Bezos appreciated the importance of thinking deeply about how to approach online retail in the early 1990s. Before starting Amazon, he invested time and effort in analysing different retail sectors and decided to start with books because he deemed them most suited to online. He could see the benefit to customers of buying books online, but was also clear on how he could make money and execute the plan from his garage, without needing to spend millions building warehouses or buying stock.

I've observed that the secret to online shopping success is finding a way to solve simultaneously three challenges which are often in conflict with each other. I call these the three pillars of online shopping success. They are:

1. Customer offer – creating a desirable offer
2. Operating model – building a profitable model
3. Execution – achieving execution success

Figure 7.1
The three pillars of online shopping success

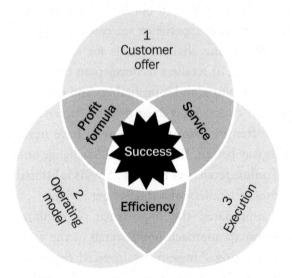

CUSTOMER OFFER

Designing the customer offer is all about assessing how best to meet your customers' needs. A good starting point is Clayton Christensen's advice to reflect on the "jobs" your customers really want done. Armed with this insight you can consider which jobs-to-be-done have the potential to be disrupted by online retail and which are best delivered through a store or other channel.

Even in a sector such as books, which has many characteristics that favour online sales, there is still a role for stores, which can thrive by focusing on particular customer needs. I'm a father of two young boys who are both learning to love reading. I know from personal experience that there are few shopping experiences as wonderful as browsing a children's bookstore together and getting advice from a knowledgeable sales assistant who can sense what sort of book the child will love. Similarly, the home delivery of books has itself been disrupted by the emergence of e-books, read on tablet devices such as Amazon's own Kindle. These are now estimated to account for 20% of all book sales.

The underlying point is that there are many reasons we may buy a book and not all will be suited to home delivery. The critical first step is to understand what these different needs are and then to work out which channel will best meet them. Bookstores coexist with e-readers and home delivery because each solution addresses different customer needs and preferences.

OPERATING MODEL

The second element that is essential to get right for an online retail business is the operating model. Walmart's experience is instructive here as it highlights the difficulty of making the right choice. After abstaining from online grocery for many years, Walmart's first attempt was a Click & Collect trial in 2011, offering pickup from local stores in its home market. It chose not to offer home delivery as it was unable to see how to make it profitable given the logistics challenges of delivering chilled fresh products. Walmart later trialled two other approaches to online grocery fulfilment: picking both from a centralised warehouse and also from its stores. More recently it acquired Jet.com, a pure-play online grocery startup looking to compete with Amazon, which operates from a warehouse and also offers third-party fulfilment. The reason Walmart had to acquire Jet.com for US\$3 billion to begin to make its mark in online is because it misjudged the situation early on and made some poor initial decisions about the best way to approach online – easy to say with the benefit of hindsight.

WAREHOUSES VS. STORES AS DISTRIBUTION CENTRES?

In the mid-1990s interest in selling products to customers through the internet was growing and Tesco was not the only company offering groceries for sale online. Its main United Kingdom competitor, Sainsbury's, had also started e-commerce home delivery and in December 1996 Sainsbury's announced it had joined forces with Hewlett-Packard for the development of an internet-based supermarket offering a full range of products. In 1995 a frozen food retailer named Iceland had already started making home deliveries as a means of combatting growing competition from the supermarkets.

All of these early entrants into online grocery sales faced a big decision when entering a market that had virtually no customers: what was the best model to adopt? Sainsbury's made the decision to pursue a warehouse-based model. Warehouse picking, in theory, had many advantages. The space was designed for picking with no regular customers to get in the way or compete for the stock on sale. However, warehouses also incurred huge setup costs which could not be recouped unless volumes were extremely high.

In the late 1990s, there were many bullish predictions about the potential impact of the internet on retail sales and Sainsbury's gambled on building expensive warehouse infrastructure to handle the demand. Despite the ambitious predictions of 1999-2001, most online grocery businesses took a very small share of the overall market and struggled to cover the fixed costs of a warehouse. Sainsbury's shut down its warehouse operation in 2001.

While Sainsbury's and numerous other retailers invested huge amounts in brand new warehouses to service the expected spike in demand that never came, Tesco adopted a more cautious approach and opted to pick directly from its network of stores. Although the stores were not designed for picking, resulting in cramped operations and challenging work practices, they had the advantage of being already paid for and physically close to the final customer. It also meant the online operation could be managed as part of the existing store teams. It was not a grandiose strategic option but it paid off big-time for Tesco. The efficiency and flexibility of the store option gave Tesco a huge head-start over its rivals.

Of course, the optimal operating model will change over time and this presents a further challenge. For example, many department store retailers chose to leverage their existing stores and stock to create a simple localised fulfilment operation. This is a simpler way to start than creating a dedicated fulfilment centre – the graveyard for many an online retailer. However, over time, as volumes grow and opportunities for automation and efficiency become significant, the optimal model evolves and centralised fulfilment will start to make more sense. Many of the department stores that started with in-store fulfilment have now migrated to central warehouses in key locations.

Figure 7.2 highlights this. It shows the trade-off between volume and cost for three different operating models available to a department store with an online business. In the early days of the business, when volumes are low, option A is the most efficient. This might be the option that leverages the retailer's existing store assets. As sales grow and the operation starts to outgrow the existing stores, the retailer transitions to option B. This might be a mixed model in which fast-moving lines are fulfilled centrally and slow-moving products continue to be picked from stores to reduce the expensive burden of holding these stocks centrally. Beyond a certain point, it makes sense to move to option C, full centralised fulfilment, which is much more efficient but incurs very high fixed costs that can now be shared over increased sales.

Figure 7.2
Different operating models may be right at different times
Illustrative cost per unit of different online fulfilment models

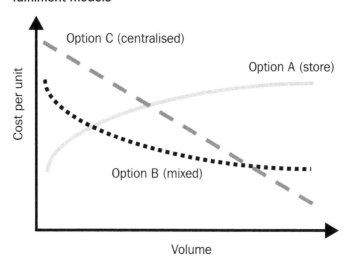

EXECUTION

A good business model combines a smart customer offer and a suitable operating model in its design. This is the profit formula that sets up an opportunity to make money. Execution makes it happen; delivering the service and efficiency that results in actual profits. It's rare to see business leaders who can both design a sound business model and then efficiently execute it. I noticed early on in my retail career with Tesco that most online leaders fell into one of two quite different camps.

At one end of the scale were leaders who had spent their careers working in stores alongside the frontline teams who served customers. This group tended to have a practical mindset and their instinct was to come up with a plan and take action. They were execution-focused.

At the other end of the scale were leaders with professional backgrounds, such as strategy consulting, who had been paid to solve problems by thinking. This group tended to have a conceptual mindset and their instinct was to understand what was happening through logic and analysis. They were focused on the profit formula.

Over the years since I've seen how these two different groups with their diverse backgrounds can come up against significant communication challenges and suboptimal results when they work together. Yet both perspectives are needed to be successful and online retailers need to find ways to integrate the two approaches in order to win. I have to admit that for a long time I didn't see Amazon as a hands-on, execution-focused retailer. From the outside all I could see was the great website. Then I read Brad Stone's book *The Everything Store*[11], which tells the story of Amazon from its very earliest years. In the mid- to late-1990s, Amazon faced huge peaks in volumes at Christmas times. Its production facilities would struggle to cope with the spike in demand and there was a risk its customers would not get their Christmas orders. For several years the team from the Amazon support office would spend the period before Christmas working in their production facilities, doing whatever it took to get the orders processed and sent to customers ready for Christmas.

As a store manager for Tesco, I also faced similar challenges on a smaller scale as we operated our own online fulfilment centre directly from the store. If online order volumes spiked higher than expected, or drivers or staff were unexpectedly absent from work, it would fall to the rest of the store team to get the job done. More than a few times I remember calling my wife to let her know I'd be home late as I set off to make deliveries around the wet and windy streets of north London because a driver had not turned up for work that day. This is a key part of execution: the willingness to get the job done no matter what it takes – an often-underestimated secret ingredient for many online retailers.

---

11 Brad Stone, *The Everything Store: Jeff Bezos and the Age of Amazon* (Little, Brown and Company, 2013).

TESCO'S SIMPLE APPROACH TO ONLINE GROCERY

At the start of this book, I told the story of Tesco's online service which was founded on the insight that customers might prefer the convenience of shopping for groceries from home. Alongside the technology team developing the application there was also an operations team who had to work out the best way to pick, pack and deliver the products to customers. The team Tesco assembled was made up of store veterans who had spent years working on the frontline and understood that an operations-based business would only succeed if it was simple for the team members who actually did the work of serving customers.

As well as making the right operating model decision about the fulfilment location, the Tesco team also spent a long time working with the frontline team members to develop the equipment they would use to execute the plan. The designs of the picking trolleys and the delivery vans were developed based on ideas from the teams who would actually do the work. The easy-to-manoeuvre picking trolley designed by a front-line team member is still in use over 20 years later and was copied by many other online grocery retailers around the world. It was this relentless focus on making it simple for the teams who did the work that meant Tesco could operate more efficiently and make fewer mistakes. Gary Sargeant, an early head of Tesco.com, visited one of Webvan's warehouses when the company's valuation was US$5 billion. Sargeant knew immediately the business wasn't going to succeed because the warehouse design did not make life simple for the teams who had to do the work. As an example, most of the female employees had to stand on crates to operate the equipment. This meant that over the course of a long shift they were more prone to make mistakes and grow tired, slowing down their productivity, as well as being put at greater risk of injury. Webvan went bankrupt just a few months after Sargeant's visit – the cost of re-work and fixing errors for customers was one of the contributory factors. Oftentimes, I see processes designed in isolation, without the involvement of the team members who will deliver the service to customers, leading to a gap between the strategic vision and what is delivered in practice.

THE SECRET TO SUCCESS

This chapter has identified the three pillars that make an online retail business successful. Within each retail sector there may be different solutions depending on the customer segment and its particular needs. We have seen huge advances in meeting the challenge of the last mile in sectors such as books and electronics. Online sales are now more than one-quarter of all retail sales in these sectors in many countries. However, there are also sectors where online has barely had an impact. Nevertheless, the secret to success in these areas will be exactly the same – a combination of an appealing customer offer, profitable operating model and successful execution.

In the next chapter I discuss some of the different online retail business models that I believe will be successful over the coming years.

CHAPTER 8

WHO WILL WIN THE RACE TO THE DOORSTEP?

Continued technology and business-model innovation will drive more and more sectors to an online tipping point. In this section I look at business models that offer a sustainable balance of a desirable customer offer and profitable operating model. There is room for more than one successful model. Variations in geography, the physical nature of products and shopping habits will mean that different approaches can be successful even in the same market.

THE EVERYTHING STORE

There's only one place to start a chapter about online retail business models: Amazon. The story of Jeff Bezos and Amazon is already extraordinary and the next two decades have the potential to dwarf what has already been achieved, not just in America but also globally.

Amazon already has operations in several other countries, including the United Kingdom, Germany, India and China. However, the United States is furthest advanced and gives the best indication of how things could evolve.

In the face of Amazon's seemingly constant announcement of incremental innovations it's hard to see what's really going on and make sense of Amazon's long-term vision. For those outside the company the pace of innovation at Amazon can be overwhelming, especially for store retailers who have belatedly realised Amazon is a major threat. Below are just a few of the innovations announced by Amazon during late 2016:

- First in-house air cargo plane for the United States market
- Free one-hour delivery of restaurant meals for Prime Now customers in several United States cities
- Launch of Amazon Echo voice-activated in-home command device in Europe
- Partnership with the United Kingdom government to explore safe ways to deliver small parcels to customers' houses using drones
- Launch of Amazon Vehicles, a car research destination and automotive community

These are just a small selection of initiatives that have been publicly confirmed. For those competing against Amazon, or who just want to understand what's really going on, it can be hard to see the big picture behind this blizzard of technology innovation and assaults on completely new markets, far removed from the original focus on books. Let's take a step back and look at Bezos's long-term vision for the future of retail.

In the early 1990s, Bezos started Amazon because he had complete belief in the power of the internet to transform shopping. In the early years of Amazon, Bezos referred to the era as "Day 1 for the internet" in his 1997 letter to shareholders. By that, he meant we were still a long way from the end-point of the impact of the internet on retail. Sixteen years later, Bezos still believed it was early days for the internet – even in 2013:

"We are still thinking of this as Day 1. In fact, I think the alarm clock is still on and we haven't even hit the snooze button yet."

JEFF BEZOS

The point is that Amazon takes an extremely long-term view. A helpful way to understand the long-term potential of Amazon is to look at the company not just as a retailer but also as an infrastructure business. In this respect, it's similar to one of the early railway or electricity pioneers described earlier. The economic model for the early developers of the railways was to lay down a huge investment at the start, with the hope of a long-term return because the railway network asset is extremely convenient for customers and difficult or impossible to copy. It took many years of hard work by tens of thousands of people to lay down the early railways, at huge financial and personal cost. At the time many commentators doubted the vision of the railway pioneers and forecast railways would never make money, or become a popular method to transport goods or people. From my perspective, Amazon is looking to achieve the modern-day equivalent of building an entirely new network of infrastructure. It is seeking to emulate as a single company the collective and nationwide achievements of many pioneering railway companies. Few other retailers seem to have noticed the true scale of its ambition.

In the United States Amazon now has an estimated 96 fulfilment centres. In a 2016 study, Gene Munster of Piper Jaffray estimated that the locations of Amazon's fulfilment centres were within twenty miles of 44% of the United States population[12]. As of July 2016, Amazon also had an estimated 63 million paying Prime customers, an increase of 19 million on 12 months earlier. Its customer base had access to a range of more than 12 million in-house and 350 million third-party vendor products.

The combination of well-located fulfilment centres, a huge range of in-house and third-party products and millions of subscription customers creates a model that will be extremely hard to compete with. The key ingredient that allows Amazon to achieve this is scale: if Amazon can reach a scale where it is sending trucks to every neighbourhood almost every day, it has created a "natural monopoly" infrastructure that allows it to make extremely efficient deliveries at low marginal cost. It will

---

12 Gene Munster, *Fulfillment Scale Should Drive A Decade Of FCF Leverage* (Piper Jaffray, 2016).

have solved the last-mile challenge across a number of retail sectors. The approach even addresses the need for urgent same-day deliveries and yet uses the efficient "milk run" logistics model.

There is a view based on conventional wisdom that Amazon is unprofitable and has only survived thanks to the willingness of investors to provide it with capital without making a profit. These criticisms are true but miss the point about the long-term goal Amazon is looking to achieve. It's a high-risk stock to own but the conventional wisdom has been wrong about Jeff Bezos and Amazon for 25 years and I wouldn't bet against him over the next 25. In the race to the doorstep, Amazon is the firm favourite.

What will limit Amazon's reach? Of course, it's hard to know how far Amazon will innovate in the years to come, but I believe this model will be increasingly successful where there is predictability to what consumers want to buy. For the typical consumer, much of our spending on big categories such as groceries, clothes and small electronics reflects what we have bought in the past. This gives online retailers an advantage because they can start with a suggested order that reflects our past purchases and consumption and then give us the option to amend it. If my family buys one packet of dishwasher tablets roughly every four weeks, then Amazon can reduce the need for me to even think about the next purchase. This smart thinking on consumers' behalf will be taken to the next level if the dishwashing machine is connected and can communicate how many cycles it has been through, placing the order for dishwasher tablets slightly earlier or later depending on usage. It's this market for staple products which will be the foundation for Amazon's success and it's where it currently has very little presence. And once Amazon is making a regular trip to your doorstep it then becomes very efficient to deliver other products on your shopping list.

THE KEYS TO SUCCESS

Amazon's is the highest-risk model but it's also the one which, if mastered, has the potential for total retail domination. The opportunity for competing offers in the United States may well have passed, but in other geographies, there is still potential for mass-market retailers with a huge appetite for innovation and investment to chase this potential pot of gold. Amazon has provided a blueprint for you to follow:

- Heavy upfront investment in infrastructure (think railways)
- Access to a complete range of products, including fresh grocery
- Seamless digital decision-making process for customers

THE VIRTUAL RETAILER

The foundation of Amazon's success is its physical assets and infrastructure. Another online retail business model takes the opposite approach. The virtual retailer such as eBay acts as a middleman between the supplier and the customer, giving customers the freedom to choose the best of several competing options.

The virtual retailer model is also one that Amazon partly adopts through its "Fulfilment by Amazon" program where the sale is made by a third party but Amazon leverages its distribution network to offer an efficient distribution option. This is an added long-term advantage of investing upfront in a distribution network.

Although eBay and more recently Amazon have been the two leaders of virtual retail, other players with online relationships with their customers, such as Google and Facebook, also have a natural advantage thanks to their closeness to the customer at key stages of the decision process. This gives these companies a unique ability to make personalised recommendations and intervene at critical points, using insights gained from the past behaviour of millions of other customers.

The virtual retailer model is attractive for one-off purchases or products that may not be in a local store – the long tail of products. However, the model will struggle to compete with the likes of Amazon's offer of staple low-margin products where the decision about what to buy is simple and what really matters is delivery efficiency.

As well as flexibility over which retailer to use, we are also seeing the emergence of business models that provide flexibility over the logistics provider for the last-mile delivery. There is potential for a new generation of virtual logistics providers who can connect customers with the best provider for each particular transport "job-to-be-done". In the United States companies such as Deliv are seeking to specialise in particular niches such as same-day delivery, which traditional courier companies can do but often at a prohibitive cost. In Australia disruptive new players like MeeMeep are emerging, looking to act as a trusted middleman between customers and logistics providers by tailoring the offer to reflect the needs of each situation. Often the intermediary can match customers with carriers with spare capacity at different times of the day or week. It's a sharing model that can be extremely efficient, as seen in other sectors such as accommodation and taxis.

THE KEYS TO SUCCESS

The beauty of the virtual model is that it frees up the retailer to focus on what it does best. The virtual retailer does not need to invest in physical infrastructure and can concentrate on really understanding its customers' needs and how they can best be solved. The network of suppliers selling through the virtual retailer can focus on product quality and service without needing to spend time and resources on marketing and awareness.

The keys to success for the virtual retailer:
• Huge traffic to its website or platform
• Deep understanding of the customer base
• Customer rating system

The key to success for suppliers to the virtual retailer:
• Compliance with different virtual retailer frameworks
• Consistent high-quality service
• Ruthless efficiency to be price-competitive

DIRECT-FROM-SUPPLIER

There have always been industries where manufacturers retail directly to the public, often through non-traditional channels or direct-to-customer outlets. This approach has traditionally suited artisan models such as bakeries where the physical production of the product can be co-located with the retail store to save time and ensure the product is fresh. However, the dominant store retail model has been to present the products of many different manufacturers, allowing customers the option of choosing from several alternatives and also making the overall shopping trip simpler. Online retail has the potential to change dramatically the economics of direct-to-customer sales by manufacturers.

The advantage to the manufacturer of a direct relationship with the end customer is that it now owns the relationship, and potentially can charge closer to the retail price than wholesale price. Some early examples of this approach have been vineyards selling wine direct to customers. This also highlights how the supplier-direct model can save money by cutting out steps in the distribution chain.

This could be an elegant solution for suppliers with loyal customers who are looking for simpler ways to buy quality products that really make a difference to their lives. An obvious opportunity would be repeat orders in sectors such as cosmetics. If the customer is already loyal to one brand of foundation, for example, a regular order to the home could be delivered cheaply via the mail, making life simpler for the customer who is saved the chore of visiting a store to make a purchase for which the decision was already made.

THE KEYS TO SUCCESS

For the direct-from-supplier model to work, the ideal segment will display some or all of three characteristics:

- Relatively high involvement in the purchase so the customer is willing to invest time in a one-to-one relationship with the supplier
- Predictable orders and brand loyalty to create a subscription-type model
- Efficient delivery options

THE SPECIALIST RETAILER

Just as store retail has a natural split between generalist retailers (department stores and supermarkets) and specialists who focus on one market niche (bakers, butchers, etc.), this mix of models will also exist in the online world. The challenge for specialist retailers is that their lack of scale makes it hard to compete on price with the likes of Amazon or eBay. The specialist model that will likely do best in the long-term therefore is a premium or highly convenient service. Some examples include specialist online retailers such as Dollar Shave Club and Diapers.com (acquired by Amazon) which have both tailored business models for customers with predictable needs. For the premium market, there are already many specialist retailers carving out a niche thanks to a vast range or specialist knowledge that is hard for a generalist online retailer to replicate.

THE KEYS TO SUCCESS

The specialist model works best in sectors where customers are looking for a quality product or a high level of service or advice. This approach is all about serving customers who are willing to pay more for a service they value. The keys to success in this model are:
• Specialist knowledge
• Curating a range that the customer trusts
• Sufficient profit margin to cover the cost of delivery

AND ONE FOR THE FUTURE: 3D PRINTING

Although this book is about online retail there is another distribution model emerging that has the potential to disrupt all of these because it takes the concept of customer convenience to a whole new level: 3D printing in the home. Footwear manufacturer New Balance recently released the Zante Generate, the first-ever shoe with a 3D printed insole. The insole can be customised to the exact fit of the individual buying the shoe. Although this version was 3D printed in New Balance's factory, the underlying convenience of this customised and almost instantaneous delivery makes me think that over time 3D printers will slowly disrupt both manufacturing and retail as they become commonplace in our homes.

CHAPTER 9

HOW TO RESPOND?

While the disruption of store retail is good news for consumers and successful new online players, it's a major challenge for retailers whose entire business model was founded on operating a physical network of stores. For retailers facing such massive change, it has proven hard to know where to start or what to do. Although many have benefited from their existing supplier and customer relationships to grow significant online sales, few have been successful in finding sustainable and profitable ways to deliver this new mode of shopping. At the same time many traditional retailers have gone out of business as the first trickle of online innovation eventually became a flood of disruption.

Learning from those who have gone before, and applying Christensen's insights about the typical course of a disruptive innovation, I have developed a simple three-step process that can help retailers map out a way to respond:

1. Understand your customers' jobs-to-be-done
2. Design **your** optimal operating model (or withdraw gracefully)
3. Execute by making life simple for the people who do the work

UNDERSTAND YOUR CUSTOMERS' JOBS-TO-BE-DONE

One of the key messages of this book (for which I am heavily indebted to the work of Clayton Christensen) is that there is a crucial step, which almost every disrupted business misses, of understanding the specific "jobs" your customers need doing. This information will then point to which jobs are best done online and which in-store. Identifying jobs-to-be-done is different from the traditional approach of looking at customer segments by characteristics such as age, income and products bought. In fact, one customer can have several jobs-to-be-done, depending on their situation at different times. Despite incumbent retailers' natural advantages, in the long run this is the only way to compete with disruptive new entrants who target customers' specific needs and gradually tempt them away with a superior offer.

To understand this point, let's consider the case of buying clothes, which already has a moderate share of online sales. If I reflect on my own needs, there are several situations in which I may need to buy clothes:

1. I know in advance exactly what I want to buy. Perhaps I'm looking for a repeat purchase of a brand and size I've been happy with in the past, for example, socks, jeans or a work shirt.
2. I'm looking for inspiration for an outfit for a special event such as a wedding or important party. I want to be 100% confident that I've made a good choice and would like to try on a few outfits and get feedback from people who have more style sense.
3. I've improved my diet and been working out at the gym and my size has gone down. I need to buy replacement clothes in the same brand but in a smaller size. I may need to try them on to be sure of the fit.
4. I'm looking to refresh my wardrobe, maybe for a change in season or because I'm going on holiday. I know roughly what I need, but I'm not fixed on particular brands or colours.
5. Something unexpected has happened and I urgently need a replacement. To take a real example, last week my trainers were stolen and I needed a replacement pair to attend a class at the gym in the evening.

Some situations, or "jobs-to-be-done", lend themselves naturally to an online purchase and home delivery. If I already know exactly what I want and there's no urgency about when I get it, it is likely to be more convenient to get it delivered to the home without my having to visit a store. Over time these sorts of simple repeat purchases will inevitably shift from stores to home delivery. This alone would cause a huge shift in many sectors. Equally, it seems less likely that I will choose to shop online for a special occasion outfit where I need to be certain that it will look right and fit me, and am looking for some style advice in the mix.

For each of these situations there is a different underlying "job-to-be-done" and the best solution will be different. All store retailers need to prepare for a future where simple repeat purchases will be transacted online and delivered to the home, possibly without the customer even being aware of the order. Much of the confusion about the potential for online retail arises because we don't break the problem down to this level of detail. We're working at too high a level of abstraction and then being caught unawares as disrupters target specific opportunities.

DESIGN YOUR OPTIMAL OPERATING MODEL (OR WITHDRAW GRACEFULLY)

At the time this book was written in 2016, the preferred strategy for store retailers around the world is to pursue an omni-channel strategy. The typical goal is to set up an operating model that makes it as simple as possible for customers to shop with the retailer, however they like and wherever they like. The managing director of John Lewis in the United Kingdom, the global benchmark for a department store omni-channel retailer, described the ideal situation, where the operation is so integrated customers don't even think about which channel they are shopping from:

> *"We know that about 60% of our customers buy both online and in shops so the approach is to make it absolutely seamless for them to move from one to the other. So they can research in one place and shop in the other, they can buy in one place and pick up in the other – the art of sales is consistent across channels, so the whole approach is to make it channel agnostic. They're not even supposed to know or see or realise which channel they're using because it's one overall customer offer."*
> ANDY STREET, JOHN LEWIS MD (2013)

This is a desirable goal, borne out of a desire to be customer-centric, rather than channel-centric, since the customer does not necessarily care which channel the retailer uses; they just want to shop in the way that is right for them. However, as with understanding the customer, there is a crucial and often-missed step for retailers who want to avoid being disrupted. They need to align their operations with the specific jobs-to-be-done best delivered in each channel. It all comes back to understanding fully why customers choose to use the different channels for different jobs and ensuring that the operating model for each channel is set up to deliver what customers want. If this step is missed, store retailers risk slowly losing sales to disruptive business models that specifically target each opportunity.

To illustrate, let's return to the example of grocery. Using the jobs-to-be-done approach highlights that a big online opportunity will be for products where customers already know in advance what they want to buy or potentially could even be advised ahead of time what they are likely to need. Online grocery retailers should be focused on making it as simple as possible for customers to re-order these sorts of products and then delivering them efficiently. Conversely, store retailers might want to shift their emphasis towards jobs-to-be-done less suited to the online channel, for example extremely urgent purchases where proximity to the customer and speed are paramount[13].

As well as thinking about how to change their offer to reflect the jobs that will be done online versus in-store, store retailers also need to work out how to develop a delivery capability that can match pure-play online retailers. In the United States, for those looking to compete directly with Amazon, it already looks like it will be hard to match the infrastructure Amazon has built. However, in other countries, there is still opportunity to develop a competitive model, able to fight off Amazon's potential entry, particularly if larger retailers are willing to partner or use the virtual retail model to extend their range. Fresh grocery is a central part of any offer modelled on Amazon's "everything store" approach: capturing customers' grocery spend provides a huge advantage because the size and frequency of grocery purchases create a barrier to entry once customers are locked into your model.

---

13 This point is discussed in detail in Christensen and Wessels, "Surviving Disruption" (*Harvard Business Review*, December 2012).

DON'T FORGET TO MAKE A PROFIT

Another common pitfall I see is that many retailers prioritise the customer when developing their customer offer and operating model, at the expense of profitability. It might seem odd to discuss the importance of profitability when Amazon, the global leader in online retail, has made notoriously little profit in the history of its retail business. Yet to my mind Amazon has a clear strategy for profitability: it's all about scale. And with hundreds of millions of customers and a vast network of infrastructure, it seems to be well on its way to achieving its goal. However, even the hope of online retail profitability has been elusive for many pure-play and store retailers.

Many models pursue the goal of a great customer offer without fully considering the cost. However, there are often ways to make slight tweaks to the customer offer that can make a material difference to profitability without damaging customer satisfaction. In the early days of Tesco.com, chief technology officer Mike McNamara encouraged us to trial small changes to the pricing of delivery on different days of the week to incentivise customers to place orders when the operation was less busy. This reduced the pressure at peak times and increased utilisation when the operation was quiet. Although there was a reduction in average delivery income per order, overall the operation was significantly ahead. In fact, sales went up because there was more free capacity on busy days for the customers who really needed those slots. Finding a way to balance customer choice and efficiency is critical to online retail success.

MAKE LIFE SIMPLE FOR THE PEOPLE WHO DO THE WORK

The final element to get right to avoid being disrupted by a new model is the execution of the plan. Many store retailers fall down here because successful execution in the online retail world is so vastly different from effective execution in stores. Executing a process-based online model is more akin to running an efficient manufacturing plant and has little in common with executing a service-based, face-to-face traditional store retail model. The skills and attitudes required are very different. Satisfying the demand from customers in the online operation, for example, requires near-perfect inventory accuracy to ensure promises made to customers online can be delivered. Contrast this with the hurly-burly of daily life in a store where good-enough inventory accuracy is often okay to run the store profitably and satisfy customers. The systems required for each model are also very different. E-commerce requires agile and proactive software and ways of working whereas many store retailers work on legacy, inflexible systems where the overriding concern is to keep the systems running.

The most important element of execution, however, is making it simple for the teams who do the work to serve customers. The cause of many execution failures is when the managers who build the strategy don't think about making life simple for the teams on the front-line, for example, my earlier story of former Webvan employees having to stand on crates to reach the equipment they used to pick products.

A NOTE ON THE ROLE OF STORES

This book is about the growth of online retail. The corollary is, of course, what will the growth of online mean for the future of stores? I see a huge amount of confusion and well-meaning but bad advice on this point, with grand conclusions about the future of stores drawn from isolated examples or anecdotes.

A key point of this book is to start by looking at the customer and their jobs-to-be-done. There will always be jobs-to-be-done more suited to stores. In fact, a number of pure-play online retailers have opened stores. Amazon has recently announced a move into local convenience stores and has even come full circle and opened several bookstores in the United States. For customers unsure about buying a new piece of Amazon technology, for example, a Kindle or the Echo voice-activated console, a store with well-informed team members is probably the best way to convert the customer. The physical presence is also an additional marketing tool: the store openings have already garnered Amazon a lot of publicity.

An analogy here would be the history of different modes of transport. The emergence of air travel over the last one hundred years has had a profound impact on previously dominant forms of travel, in particular trains and boats. But we've not seen these modes of travel disappear. Instead, they have evolved and adapted to cater to the jobs-to-be-done for which they are most suited. Just sixty years ago the most popular way to travel from the United Kingdom to Australia was by boat, the journey taking several weeks. Today, almost all personal travel to Australia is by plane, with the 15,000 to 17,000 kilometre trip from the United Kingdom taking only 24 hours. However, air transport has had a relatively minor impact on the freight of manufactured goods: sea transport remains the most efficient way to transport non-urgent freight over long distances. It will be the same with the evolution of retail. The secret to the survival of retail stores is to spot the jobs that stores do best and focus on delivering those.

As the online channel evolves and satisfies more of our jobs-to-be-done, the overall trend will be for stores to have a much smaller role as a product distribution hub. Their function will increasingly be to provide the elevated experiential service that shopping at home cannot provide. Of course, there will still be many situations where products are stored and sold from stores but if this reduces by another 10 to 20 percentage points from current levels over the next few years, the impact will be dramatic. The Apple store is a model here: very high sales per square metre on a small footprint and much of the product dispatched from a central warehouse.

Another oft-talked about trend is for stores to become local distribution centres, leveraging their proximity to customers and existing range of products. Many commentators talk about the advantage store retailers have over pure-play online because they can use their existing stores as warehouses. Using stores as warehouses also gives access to the products sitting only on store shelves and not in the warehouse.

As a short-term option, using stores as distribution centres makes sense as a way to get started and leverage existing assets. I spent several years working to develop and improve Tesco.com's store-based online grocery model, before the market was large enough to support a centralised warehouse. There are also specific situations where store-based fulfilment can be a winning strategy. For example, some shopping mall owners in the United States now support their tenant retailers by co-ordinating their deliveries through one preferred transport provider. By collaborating, the mall-based retailers gain economies of scale and can potentially offer the holy grail of cheap same-day delivery to customers who live close to the mall.

However, for mass-market retailers looking to meet customers' everyday shopping needs, using stores as distribution centres will struggle to compete against the efficiency of an automated, centralised distribution centre as volume increases. A common pitfall is that variable costs incurred are treated as fixed or not even measured. Often it can be hard to track and measure exactly what costs are incurred by the online business, especially when resources are shared. To take an example, imagine a customer visits an online department store and orders a product with a retail value of $20. If the retailer paid $10 for the product, which is now sitting on the shelves in one of its stores, and can pack and mail it to the customer for $6, they'll book a $4 profit to the online business. It looks like everyone is ahead, especially the retailer who may have directed the order to a store where the product was not selling well and would otherwise have been sold at a markdown.

In isolation the sale makes sense. However, I've seen again and again that the costs incurred earlier in the chain are often unaccounted for. As online grows it is possible for volumes to reach 10%, 15% or even 20% of the store's total sales. At this level, the true end-to-end costs of supporting online sales could easily be more than the $4 notional profit per sale. The biggest hidden cost is often the supply chain cost of the distribution centres and logistics that delivered the product to the store. This is illustrated in figure 9.1 – many profit and loss statements for the online operations of store retailers exclude the supply chain costs incurred before the products reach the store.

Figure 9.1
Not all costs get counted in online retail P&Ls

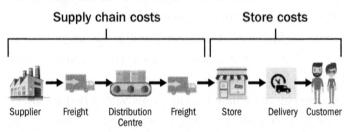

As online volumes increase many retailers also find there can be significant flow-on effects to the rest of the store operation, for example from the online shopping team who are busy picking the products from shelves to fulfil online orders and impacting the shopping experience of in-store customers. All these things will start to affect the company's overall bottom line, even if it is not directly measured. For retailers who have not been investing in a centralised online fulfilment capability, once their online sales hit the volumes suggested above they will find it hard to compete with the likes of Amazon in the United States, or John Lewis in the United Kingdom, who have invested heavily in efficient centralised fulfilment for their online businesses.

In my opinion, the John Lewis model is the optimal long-term foundation for a retailer looking to be strong in both online and store retail. John Lewis has set up one centralised fulfilment centre that is able to service both its stores and its online customers. The secret was a large investment in automation technology that allows flexible picking: the same equipment and infrastructure can fulfil a single product ordered by a customer for home delivery or a large order of the same product for one of its busiest stores. John Lewis now has one third of its sales coming through the online channel.

CONCLUSION

---

*"If you defer investing your time and energy
until you see that you need to, chances
are it will already be too late."*
CLAYTON CHRISTENSEN

History has a tendency to repeat itself. Each time a disruptive online retail model emerges, most retailers overlook its significance until it's too late. To prepare for the future, we need to understand the forces driving consumers to shop in completely new ways and be ready to react when a disruptive opportunity emerges.

It starts with thinking about the customer, the jobs they need doing, and the way an individual retail sector is likely to evolve to meet their needs. I've presented a framework to understand the last-mile challenge, by breaking the problem down into its two key components:

decision and delivery. Although every product category will be different, there are underlying principles emerging that can be applied across sectors.

The biggest obstacle for most retailers is finding the time to think about and focus on long-term goals when just managing today's world is so tough. To avoid being a victim of disruptive innovation, however, there is no alternative.

For retailers, time is running short to think, act and get ahead of the huge changes to come.

ARTICLES AND BOOKS
I RECOMMEND

"What is Disruptive Innovation?"
Clayton M. Christensen, Michael E. Raynor,
Rory McDonald
Harvard Business Review, December 2015

Consumer Delivery Preferences Report
Blackbay and MeeMeep, 2016

The Everything Store: Jeff Bezos and the Age of Amazon
Brad Stone
Little, Brown and Company, 2013

Management in 10 Words
Terry Leahy
Random House Business, 2012

"Surviving Disruption"
Clayton M. Christensen, Maxwell Wessels
Harvard Business Review, December 2012

Mindset: The New Psychology of Success
Carol S. Dweck
Random House, 2006

GRATITUDE

Thanks to the leaders and members of the Thought Leaders Business School who inspired me to write a book.

For supporting me in my retail career, thanks to those I worked alongside at Tesco, Coles Supermarkets and Aussie Farmers Direct and the clients in my consulting business, including the wonderful people at Myer, the leading Australian department store. There have been too many people to call out individually but I owe a huge debt of gratitude to the leaders at Tesco who supported my secondment to be the store manager of the Brent Cross superstore in north London, taking a risk on a head office analyst to run one of Tesco's toughest shops.

For support with this book, thanks to my patient and supportive writing mentor, Kath Walters. Also to subeditor Jaclyn McRae, book designer Lorna Hendry, and artist Steph Hughes, who created a cover illustration that captured exactly what I had in mind.

Thanks to the friends who supported me along the way and my family in England: Nick, Mel, Bertie and Theo, and my parents.

Last but not least, to my own amazing family: Anna, Leo and Max, who have been patient and understanding while I was locked away writing this book.